S0-CWP-929

Table of Contents

Foreword

In November, 1993, President Clinton signed into law a bill that makes it more difficult for federal and state governments to enact laws that infringe on religious practices. This legislation overturns a 1990 Supreme Court case that gave government more power in protecting victims of organizations operating in the name of religious freedom. The Court decision had stated that government could infringe on religious freedoms when a valid public purpose was served and when inhibiting religion was not the main goal. In signing the 1993 bill, President Clinton stated that "our laws and institutions should not impede or hinder, but rather protect and preserve fundamental religious liberties. What this law basically says is that the government should be held to a very high level of proof before it interferes with someone's free exercise of religion. This judgment is shared by the people of the United States as well as by the Congress."

While President Clinton should be applauded for urging Americans to return to religious values to help "heal this troubled land," he must be taken to task for failing to recognize that his latest actions have provided the thousands of cults currently operating in the United States with more power to destroy those very values he is trying to protect. I have seen hundreds of innocent lives lost in the name of religious freedom and religious values, merely because those people honestly believed they were following a Divine Shepherd. They could not see that they were being victimized by mind control techniques that instructed them to surrender to death. Complete and accurate information would have allowed them to make a healthy, intelligent choice of convictions.

Because of the current political climate that inadvertently gives further protection, hence encouragement, to destructive cults, a counterbalance is needed to protect the innocent from falling victim to the misguided and misguiding, self-proclaimed prophets who establish and perpetuate those cults. The counterbalance is education. Through education of the masses, cults are less able to disguise their hideous secrets, to mask their lies, and to inflict their paralyzing mind control techniques.

Alice Scott became the victim of a destructive cult, the Branch Davidians, when her son innocently chose to follow the teachings of David

Koresh. In her effort to help her son recover from the damaging effects of the cult, Alice undertook an intensive, four-year research project to understand how cults operate. That research alone could fill volumes. But Alice condensed her findings into a succinct, easy-to-read manuscript that will help others understand what cults are and how they operate. Blue River Publishing Inc. is proud to publish that manuscript, *The Incredible Power of Cults*.

—Jim Scheetz, Publisher

Introduction

One of the bittersweet pleasures of being a parent is having a child reach adulthood and leave the nest, armed with all the love and guidance that you have provided for twenty-something years. The bitter is in the parting, the feeling of loss because you are no longer needed as protector, provider and nurturer. The sweet is in the pride of knowing that you have done a good job, that a part of you is going out into the world.

So it was in February, 1989, when my son Robert completed technical school and left for California, a new career, and a new life. He was twenty-six, strong-bodied and handsome. Tucked into his briefcase was his degree in avionics (with honors!) and a lucrative job offer. But what gave me the most pride was what was tucked into his head—self-confidence, lofty goals, esteem, and a great deal of moral integrity. I could not have been more proud.

My world was shattered when nine months later Robert was deposited by private plane at the small, charter airport in Colorado Springs, ten miles from our home. I nearly mistook him for a stranger. His clothes were worn and crumpled. His face was sunken, pale and unshaven. His hair was long and matted. He looked like an older-generation bridge-person; tired, dirty, and defeated. And when I hugged him, he smelled like a sewer rat. He acknowledged me briefly but with total detachment as he stared into space, connecting with, and communicating with, images or entities invisible to me. My son returned to me a stranger.

The day before I had been warned by David Koresh (he called himself Vernon Howell then) that he was sending Robert home because "he is going in and out of reality." At the time I knew very little about cults in general, and nothing about the Branch Davidians of which David was the leader. But when I met my son at the airport, I vowed I would investigate and understand how one person, or a group of persons, could within a period of a few months, capture and destroy the mind of another perfectly healthy human being.

Within hours, Robert was bathed and dressed in fresh-laundered clothes. But the vacant stare remained in his eyes. It would be another four years before Robert would fully return to us mentally.

During that time Robert received extensive professional therapy and counseling. To better understand what he had gone through and to help in his recovery, I learned as much as I could about cults, especially the Branch Davidians. I discovered and contacted cult awareness and research organizations, cult experts, psychiatrists, psychologists, former cult members, even police departments, methodically entering everything into a journal. I had more conversations with David Koresh. I spent days at the library, reading books about cults and mind control. I sought help from pastors and church members. And each time I felt I had reached my limit in frustration, another clue or solution would be given to me to reaffirm my determination. The healing process, both for my son and myself, seemed endless, but eventually proved effective.

Then in February, 1993, came news of the raid by federal agents on the Branch Davidian compound in Waco, Texas where my son had stayed for several weeks. Four agents and six Davidians were killed, leading to a 51-day standoff between the agents and a group of people who thought they answered to a higher power bestowed on their leader, the self-appointed savior-on-earth, David Koresh.

On April 19, the compound exploded in brilliant fireballs and smoke, killing David Koresh and 85 followers, including 17 children.

The siege was ended, but the nightmarish images remained. My son had survived the influence of David Koresh and his cult. But what about the millions of others who are affected, either directly or marginally, by the thousands of cults that are still active in the United States? How will they cope; how will they survive? Where can people find help? I had to put everything I know into one resource...this book.

I don't have all the answers, but perhaps the information I have struggled to compile will help others who are seeking direction and understanding in dealing with the incredible, and often devastating, power of cults.

—Alice Scott, December 1993

What is a Cult?

Cult researchers estimate that between 2500 and 7500 recognized cults currently are active in the United States, with a total membership of anywhere from 3 million to well over 10 million people, adults and children. The numbers are staggering. But why is there such a discrepancy in the numbers?

There is no universal definition of a cult. "Cult" means different things to different people. For instance, the Religious Movements Resource Center, which estimates 2500 active cults in the United States with several hundred thousand members, identifies a cult by its deceptive recruiting and indoctrination, mind control practices, violence, and general "cult-like" operation (secrecy, single truth, total obedience to the leader). Meanwhile, Watchman Fellowship, also a cult education organization, estimates that 7500 active cults are in existence with membership in the millions. They determine an organization to be a cult if it follows the mind control and ego destruction techniques outlined by Robert J. Lifton (see bibliography) and which includes control of information, mystical manipulation (divine purpose), need for purity, confession, sacred science (obedience to an only true logical system of beliefs), loading the language, doctrine over persons, and dispensing of existence (non-believers are doomed).

My definition of a cult is any organization of two or more people, where the leader persuades the followers to believe that he/she has a certain right and authority to command unconditional loyalty and obedience, to the extent that the followers, individually or collectively, will willingly act against the commonly known and accepted laws of God, nature and/or humanity to inflict mental and/or physical damage to another of God's creatures in an effort to further the cause of the group.

The severity of a cult, of course, lies in the extent to which its members will inflict harm on others, even its own members; and their inability to determine right from wrong, true from false, and good from evil, based on their unconditional trust in a leader who determines how they are to live their secret lives.

Characteristic practices of a cult

Unfortunately, there is no checklist of attributes that would identify an organization or religious group as being a cult or not a cult. If we could only identify a group as having legal or illegal practices, it would help, but our legal system today is clogged by lawsuits brought about by individuals claiming physical or mental harm caused by an organization. It is truly a fuzzy area between cult and non-cult, between legal and illegal.

The best anyone has been able to do is to determine a set of potentially harmful practices and apply them to the situation being questioned.

Here are six characteristic practices that I look for to determine whether or not an organization is a dangerous cult or engages in cult-like activities:

1. Oppressively authoritarian. — All groups have some type of leadership or they would not survive. But when that leadership becomes oppressively authoritarian, the group takes on cultish tendencies. When an organization is oppressively authoritarian, it has one leader who answers to no one else, who establishes a hierarchy of power and leadership, who allows no room for independent action or ideas, and who commands complete loyalty and obedience.

2. Exclusive. — The group professes to have exclusive knowledge about the correct path toward salvation or enlightenment. Religious cults receive this "exclusive knowledge" by divine intervention; non-religious groups receive it through the "super intelligence" of their founders.

3. "Us-versus-them" mentality. — Because they have "exclusive knowledge," cults set themselves apart from all other social institutions, including the law and (in the case of religious cults) other religious organizations. Members come to believe, therefore, that it is necessary for them to adjust and change their values, their beliefs and their actions to conform to the rules and guidelines of the organization, regardless of the rules of society.

4. Manipulative. — To attract and maintain members, cults resort to manipulation, or mind control techniques. They manipulate information, authority, time, physical appearance and reality.

5. Subjective. — Through mind control practices, cults effectively make their members stop thinking for themselves, and by concentrating on feelings and emotions, to experience the new cult reality, leaving the "thinking" to the cult leaders.

6. Secretive. — Along with the hierarchy of authority, cults maintain a hierarchy of "knowledge," which causes members to be constantly striving for "ultimate wisdom," or "the true light." This layered approach to dispensing knowledge based on a member's "worthiness" allows the cult to engage in certain practices that are either kept from members, or left unexplained (accepted on faith) until the member achieves the proper "level of worthiness."

Common misperceptions about cults

The news media is abundant with "cult" stories. Cult activities are often parlayed into megabucks in the form of increased viewership or readership. But what you usually see, hear and read about are the spectacular events such as the Waco holocaust, or the Jonestown massacre*. Another, though less spectacular, theme is child abuse. The motion picture industry often includes scenes of drug abuse, satanic rituals, and/or sexual free-for-alls. Unfortunately, if there is not a dramatic element to the story, it probably won't be reported by the news. Therefore, there are many misperceptions about what a cult is or does. These are the most common:

Someone like David Koresh of the Branch Davidians could never get me to follow him. In fact, no cult could ever get me to join. — Consider that of the hundreds of thousands of people who have been involved in a cult, most would have told you that they would never join a cult. The fact remains, we are all vulnerable to some extent. Consider all the things in your life that you cherish most: family, a religious belief, love, attachments, and freedom from suffering. Now consider any areas in your life that feel incomplete or unfulfilled. Be assured that of the many thousands of cults currently operating in the United States, there is one, probably many, that can quickly determine the vulnerabilities in your life and can take advantage of you, even while you firmly believe you are acting intelligently, willingly and in your best interest. Now consider, that of the millions of people that are currently involved in a cult or have been involved at one time in their lives, many felt exactly as you do before they joined the group. Your best protection from being involved in a cult is knowledge: knowledge of yourself, and knowledge of cults.

Cults use drugs to get people to join. — The truth, I have found, is that very few cults use drugs of any kind, either to get people to join, or to control the minds of those who have already joined. (The possible exception to this is the use of herbs, which is described in Section 3, page 34). Many don't even allow alcoholic beverages. Cult leaders generally rely on mind control techniques to gain power over members. Also realize that cults do not want to draw attention to themselves by breaking any laws, and illegal drugs are often a magnet for investigation by law enforcement.

Perhaps the reason for this very prevalent misperception that cults use drugs is that books and movies (fiction) that portray cult activities, pick up

---

*On November 18, 1978, more than 900 men, women and children, all followers of People's Temple founder Jim Jones, committed mass suicide at their compound in Jonestown, Guyana, South America.

11

on the dramatic manifestations of cult members who are suffering from severe mind control: vacant staring into space, talking to invisible entities, inability to function on a conscious level in the here and now. These activities are relatively rare, and when they do occur, are not easily explained as being caused by mind control. It is much easier to explain these actions as being drug induced.

Cults make people go through certain rituals in order for them to become or to remain members. — Cults do rely on certain routines for their members such as attending meetings and listening to dogma by the leader or leaders, attending to chores, and advancing the cause or belief of the organization. This can be said of many organizations not considered cults. Religious or pseudo-religious cults may even observe certain rites or rituals that are not considered "cultish." I believe the misperception arises from the activities of certain occult organizations and satanic cults. The important message here is that rites and rituals become dangerous when they activate the collective mind-set of the group to inflict harm on individuals, either inside or outside the group, or on living creatures. Generally, if potential members were subjected to harmful rites or rituals, they would not join the group.

Cults and Christians are the same. — Christians are, by virtue of their name, Christ-like. Christ was not selfish, deceptive, self-centered, manipulative or dictatorial. Cult members and leaders may be some or all of the above. Cults, however, often use religion in general, and Christianity in particular, to serve as a basis of their existence to prey upon their membership, to direct power to their leaders, and to fortify their existence by citing their right to religious freedom under the Bill of Rights to the Constitution. However, their "interpretation" of the Christian Bible is completely self-serving.

Cult members are threatened with death if they try to leave the group. — News headlines, photos and motion pictures tend to focus on the dramatic elements of cults and cult activities. What can be more dramatic than a mass suicide or a spectacular explosion? It is true that many religious cults base their beliefs on their interpretation of an inevitable "end-times" or "Armageddon"—it is one method of a leader's powerful control over the membership. Such a belief can lead to such dangerous activities as stockpiling weapons leading to a holocaust, or mind control leading to a mass suicide. Sometimes, as in the case of David Koresh and the Branch Davidians, the group is threatened by outside forces, usually law enforcement, and they resort to killing others in the name of protecting themselves.

What usually happens is that when cult members consider leaving a cult, they are threatened by the cult leader with "eternal damnation" because they have received and then rejected "the word." This is a very powerful threat; one that puts considerable mental stress on an individual who leaves such a cult. But rarely are cult members, in my opinion, actually threatened with death should they decide to leave the group.

Cults and the occult are the same. — Perhaps because the words are so similar, cults are often thought to be a part of the occult. They can be, but most are not. The occult is defined as relating to or dealing with the supernatural; mysterious or beyond human comprehension; secret, or available only to those initiated; and concealed or hidden. When speaking of the occult, most people include astrology, psychic prediction (palm reading, tarot card reading, crystal ball gazing, etc.), and sometimes magic. Many people equate the occult with satanism or devil worship; hence, satanic cults. Finally, cults and the occult often share elements such as secrecy or mysticism, but they should not be considered as one and the same.

People who join cults do so with their eyes wide open. — Another way of saying this is that people who join a cult, know beforehand exactly what they are getting into and they understand the consequences of their actions. Every former cult member that I have talked to, and those I have seen on television or heard on the radio or read about in books, have made a statement like, "If I had only known what I was getting involved in, I never would have allowed it to happen to me." It is true that we all have free will, and joining a cult is an act of free will. But cults are joined by people who like what they see about the cult, not by what is hidden from them. (Read more about this under Indoctrination, Section 3, page 27).

Cults believe in free love, free sex, free drugs and free will. — I was a young adult in the sixties and early seventies when protesting and rebelling were popular. Many developments sparked that movement: the war in Vietnam, the threat of nuclear annihilation, environmental pollution, and a general mistrust of authority. Many "cults" sprang up at that time, professing free love, free sex, free drugs and free will as a means of acting out that protest against the authority figures who were seen as responsible for the world's major problems. And many of those cult activities were reported by the news media and became themes in novels and motion pictures. I don't believe the same is true today. Yes, there may be some cults that believe in some or all of those activities, but the majority do not. But while most of those types of cults no longer exist, the images continue to linger.

Cult members could leave if they really wanted to. — This misperception is difficult to refute or to explain, because everyone has a different sense of reality, and reality for a cult member is hardly the reality that you or I have. First, I believe that the fear of possible consequences, especially the threat of eternal damnation, prevents many members from leaving a cult, even when they "really want to." Some are tied to a cult because of others who are in the cult, usually close family members. Still others have become dependent on the cult for survival—they usually have no money, no job, no family, no support system to turn to on the "outside" for protection and survival. Or, they feel that since they turned their backs on everyone on the "outside," they cannot admit their mistake, ask for forgiveness, and be accepted back into the world they knew before joining the cult. Finally, many cult members are convinced that they deserve their life on earth and in the cult, and must endure it to achieve eternal salvation.

Only a complete idiot or a mentally deranged person would follow someone like David Koresh or Jim Jones. — If you looked at the make-up of the Branch Davidians, you would find teachers, engineers, lawyers, nurses, and even former ministers. Membership in a cult is not a measure of low I.Q. In fact, just the opposite could be said. Cults do not recruit the mentally impaired. Nor do they actively recruit people of low intelligence. To serve their purposes and to advance their causes, cults prefer to concentrate on people who have a lot to offer including money, position, and intelligence. And when it comes to need in a person's life—the void which a cult seeks to fill in the members it recruits—a person's measure of intelligence is not a measure of vulnerability.

Either a cult is all good, or it is all bad; there is no in between. — Some of the good things people feel within the atmosphere of a cult are a sense of belonging, sharing a common goal among friends, having needs met (food, clothing, shelter, "spiritual" insight), and a certain discipline (structured work, study, play and diet). Strict discipline and control within a cult have been known to cure drug and/or alcohol dependency, temper emotional outbursts (forcing members to control their tempers), and in some cases, elevate self-esteem within individuals. It is these good things that lure people to join cults. The bad aspects almost always involve some form of mind control and can include sexual misconduct, lying, stealing, physical abuse, even murder or suicide. The point I am trying to make is that if a cult were all bad, no one would join, and if it were all good, it would not be considered a cult. I believe that all cults have some good and some bad attributes. It is the degree of one or the other that makes them different and more or less dangerous.

A cult can be a "family," but a family cannot be a cult. — Probably more cults are true family cults, where all the individuals are closely related (father, mother, children, grandparents, etc.) than any other type of cult. But the line between a dysfunctional family and a dangerous family cult is very fuzzy.

When one person acts as "head of household," he or she may become oppressively authoritarian, leading to such dangerous activities as child abuse, spousal abuse or parental abuse. Very often in divorce cases, children are the victims of severe mind control by one parent who attempts to discredit or invalidate the other spouse through lies and deceit. Battered women often feel powerless to get out of a marriage, and are often made to feel that they deserve their beatings. The elderly are even more vulnerable to mistreatment by their children, and are even more powerless to do something about it.

To determine if a dysfunctional family is truly a family cult, follow the list of practices on page 10 and apply them to the individual in control.

No one should be forced to endure an abusive situation. It is the purpose of this book to allow everyone to recognize a cultish, abusive situation and to understand what is happening and how. And hopefully, through knowledge and understanding, the situation can be changed.

Who is vulnerable?

Most people tell me they could never be persuaded to join a cult. Even my son felt he could never be influenced. But look what happened.

After he left his home in Colorado, Robert was without close friends and family. He had no one whom he trusted or liked well enough to share his accomplishments, his good fortunes, his concerns and his beliefs. He eventually met a young man whom he felt comfortable and open with. Jimmy was intelligent, respectful, light-hearted and caring. He was Robert's age and could relate to Robert's needs and interests. He even shared Robert's love of the Bible and all it offered including spiritual peace and enlightenment.

But Jimmy also was a follower of David Koresh. At that time, David was known as Vernon Howell, who was admired because of his very keen insight into the knowledge and meaning of the Bible. Not only had he committed scriptures to memory, he appeared to interpret with ease, all parts of the Bible and how the various parts fit together.

This group of people, who looked upon David Koresh as a religious guide, seemed loving, caring, honest and sincere. They held the same values and the same interests as Robert. And they "adopted" Robert into their fold.

The tragic fate of David Koresh and his followers in the Branch Davidian cult is well known. The part that is difficult to understand is how David's followers could be so deceived into believing he was a "savior," deceived to the point that they would commit genocide.

My son was fortunate to have left the group before the holocaust, but he knew many of the members who died in the fire, including Jimmy and of course, David Koresh, and he understands how the followers became caught up in David's world. According to Robert, it was a matter of building on belief and trust, very gradually, very carefully, until the minds of the followers were locked into the mind of David Koresh. The very same technique is used every day in the lives of every one of us—only the ends are different.

A good example of how this works is the age-old experiment of the frog in water. Put him in hot water and he will quickly jump out. But put him in comfortable water, then gradually turn up the heat, and eventually he will be cooked to perfection without his being aware of the hot water he is in.

The same thing happens to each of us in our daily lives. We place our trust and confidence in family, friends, organizations, leaders, and even products. We take back that trust and confidence when the other individual, group or object performs in a way that we oppose (the water becomes hot very quickly and we jump out of the pot). But when the trust and confidence is allowed to build over a long period of time, we tend to tolerate (or fail to recognize altogether) the gradual discomfort that the other person, group or product is causing us. The most difficult part is knowing when to get out of the water.

There seem to be two elements that determine whether or not we rid our lives of people, groups or things before they have a chance to cause harm. One is free will, the ability to choose to continue or to terminate a situation or relationship. The second is insight, the ability to recognize a situation as it is rather than as others say it is, or as we would like it to be.

How free will is lost

Free will is the freedom to choose. When discussing cults, it appears so simple to rationalize that a cult member has free will, the freedom to choose to stay in the cult or to leave. If only it were that simple! Before a person can choose his own actions, he must determine his own goals. To do that he must recognize his own values.

Cults are aware of the power of values in a person's life, especially when recruiting members. By aligning the cult's values with the prospective member's values, a cult gains the trust and confidence of a prospective member. Some of the basic values promoted by cults are truth, honesty, love of God and family, respect of the individual, providing comfort and aid.

Once values are recognized and aligned, goals are established and include enlightenment, understanding, faith and conviction. When the goals are established, actions to achieve those goals are followed. Those actions may begin innocently enough with structured meetings, diets, and rituals such as praying, meditating or worshipping.

What happens in a cult is that once the goals are set and reinforced, values and actions change to achieve those goals. Eventually, lying, cheating, stealing, physical and mental abuse, and even murder or suicide, become acceptable values if they are used to achieve the goals.

16

At this point cult members are no longer choosing their values, or even their goals and, consequently, their actions. Instead, the cult leader has subtly replaced them with the cult's values, goals and actions, and, in effect, has stolen the individual's free will.

How insight is lost

There are many cliches that deal with insight; "He couldn't see the forest for the trees," "She sees things through rose-colored glasses," and "You can't tell those people anything, they have blinders on (or tunnel vision, or a one-track mind)."

Cult members see the world with cult-colored glasses.

It is well documented that once individuals have been successfully indoctrinated into a cult and accept the cult "family," they also undergo a complete personality or identity change, with different values, thoughts and emotions. The cult becomes the new reality.

The old ideas, the old family and friends, and the old "world" become enemies which, according to the cult leader, hold the individual back from seeing "the light," reaching true enlightenment, or true understanding. Even the "rational" mind, and all its previous modes of thought, becomes discredited. The individual is taught to let go, to give in to the truth, to accept the new and only true faith or dogma.

When this happens, the new cult member will have lost both free will, and the insight to recognize that free will has been lost, or that the cult is dangerous. And no amount of intelligence—not knowledge, but intelligence—can protect a person from succumbing to cult indoctrination.

Protection from within

When David Koresh sent my son Robert home from the cult, it was because, he said, Robert was going "in and out of reality." In fact, many people who saw Robert when he came home probably thought he had "flipped out." He had the glassy stare, he talked to imaginary beings, he had lost touch with reality in that he barely, if at all, recognized people and surroundings from his life of just a few months before.

What happened is that David Koresh and the Branch Davidians were never able to reach Robert's "inner being." That "inner being" responded to protect Robert by causing him to seemingly "flip out," forcing David Koresh to send him home.

According to cult experts, this type of protection from within is not unusual. Cult members, they say, have two identities, one belonging to the cult, and one, the true identity, that is suppressed by cult indoctrination. But the true identity is never eliminated completely, and often works on a subconscious level to free the individual from the cult identity.

This suppressed "inner being" has been known to cause psychosomatic illness, from simple but persistent strange rashes to attacks of asthma or diabetes. Sometimes it will prompt the cult member to drop subtle hints to family members to rescue them from the cult. Sometimes it persuades the individual to return to a previous environment, away from the cult. In Robert's case, it caused him to lose touch with reality, which cult leader David Koresh could not deal with, and Robert was sent home.

Even as a cult member is operating under the cult identity, the "inner being" remembers right from wrong, good from bad. Cult experts report that quite often, after cultists are deprogrammed, they remember incidents of rape or physical abuse and torture, or occasions when they were forced to lie or cheat or steal, but that while they were under control of the cult identity, they were unable to act any differently. Their free will had been taken from them, or more accurately, they entrusted their free will to someone else.

Why do people get involved in cults?

What do you desire most in life? Happiness? Love? Money? Everyone wants more affection and more attention. Many want better health, more meaning in life, more wisdom and understanding, perhaps even more recognition and status. Cults promise to provide all these things.

While these wants and needs are present in all of us to some degree, certain events in our lives cause us to be more vulnerable because of these needs. Whenever there is an abrupt change in our lives, there is a distinct void that needs filling. Whether it is the death of someone close to us, a divorce, loss of a job, or even a move to another city, a lack or void is created. Cults are there, ready to fill that void.

America is also a nation of believers. We believe in family values. We believe in a need for authority, whether in our homes, our schools, or our social and political institutions. We believe in success through hard work, health through clean living, and spiritual well-being through prayer. Cults believe all these things as well!

So what happens when society disappoints us and shatters our beliefs? When we have worked hard all our lives, only to be fired from our jobs when we are fifty years old? When our respected leaders are exposed for lying, cheating and stealing? When our education system fails, or law enforcement no longer protects the innocent, or when our religious institutions seem to place undue reverence on the almighty dollar? We begin looking for other solutions, other leaders for our guidance, other institutions in which to place our faith. Ironically, cults exist because we are unable to live without faith. And they are successful because of the promises they make.

Birth of a Cult

How do cults get started? The answers are probably as many and as varied as the number of cults in existence. But they all have one thing in common—all their beginnings can be traced back to a single individual. By examining cult leaders, we can better understand how cults arise.

Because this book focuses on destructive cults, it must be stated here that not all cults are dangerous or destructive, and in fact, most cults begin with innocent, if not honorable, intentions. The problem with a cult arises when its leadership changes its focus or intent and becomes harmful.

The cult leader

Some cults change in a negative way when the leadership changes. A cult leader dies, or is ousted, and another cult member takes control. In these cases, a cult leader is "born" within a cult, rises in the ranks, and eventually takes over. At this point there is generally a great deal of upheaval; many cult members leave, and those who stay basically agree in mindset with the new leader and the cult takes off in a new direction.

But what about the person who starts a cult where before there was none?

Most people assume that cult leaders begin as experts in their field. For instance, a religious cult will begin when a minister, a missionary, or a religious zealot begins preaching a new dogma or a new interpretation of the Bible. But history proves this is not always the case.

Some very famous cult leaders began as salesmen, truck drivers, pop musicians and science fiction writers. One was even a carnival barker.

What all of these people have in common is a certain charisma, a certain salesmanship or showmanship, a certain power to persuade others. What sets them apart from other individuals who are equally charismatic, is that they become addicted to the attention and the power that others give them. They want more. Eventually, they want it all!

As the budding cult leaders continue to espouse their doctrine, their theory for living, they continue to wield influence. Others listen to them. Others follow them. Their power base begins to grow, their philosophy ex-

---

More than 50 percent of new cults fail in the first two years.

pands according to their whims or "divine revelations," and the leader's influence grows. Power becomes a drug.

As leaders gain power and influence, they also quickly learn how to manipulate people. They learn what arouses others to respond positively, what causes them to follow blindly, what causes them to put their faith in another person. They learn to push the right buttons. Whether they realize it or not, whether it was their initial intent or not, they learn mind control.

Eventually, the leaders begin to believe their own words. They become victims of the same mind control techniques they are using on others. They become convinced that they are someone special, that they have a special gift, that they are chosen, that they are—saviors!

For the leader, it is a heady trip indeed. Some become fascinated by the wealth they are able to accumulate. Others are content with the drug of power and attention and influence. Some want to test the strength of their powers, to see just how far they are able to go, and they introduce actions or behaviors into the cult such as sexual abuse. For most destructive cults, the ends justify the means and they place themselves above the law.

Other cults test their influence on politicians or on society in general and learn how to take unlawful advantage.

Many cult leaders find that their power (over a certain number of their followers at least) is absolute because their mind control techniques have been so successful. Few people, not even the President of the United States, ever achieve this kind of power!

Why do cults recruit?

Whether or not a cult recruits new members, and the extent to which a cult recruits, are generally determined by the motives of its leader. If a cult leader prefers to keep a low profile so as not to draw attention to the cult's activities, and is content with wielding power over a small group of people, recruiting will be kept to a minimum. If, however, the leader is a megalomaniac and measures his or her power and influence by the total number of followers, the cult will recruit heavily.

Some cults will recruit with the intention of influencing politicians who can establish or defeat laws that may protect the cult's existence, or to influence foreign policies such as arms dealing or drug trafficking. Therefore the cult will recruit individuals (lawyers, young politicians) who can help them influence politicians. Some target certain companies or groups of businesses that, when infiltrated and in some cases overtaken completely, will advance their goals. Some cults will recruit in direct proportion to the amount of wealth they want to accumulate.

Some cults recruit individuals who can legitimize their group (other religious leaders, teachers, politicians or law enforcement members), or to cover their faults (e.g., recruiting doctors to cover allegations of physical mistreatment, or lawyers who can defend them in court).

For whatever reason or to whatever extent a cult recruits, recruiting serves to reaffirm cult members' belief in themselves and their goals.

Who are the recruiters and how do they recruit?

Recruitment by a cult for new members may be passive or active. Usually smaller cults that are less interested in enlarging their membership, do not actively recruit, but rather let potential new members come to them. This usually happens when friendships develop between members and non-members, and the non-member shows interest in the group, asks questions, and shows a desire to attend one of the group's meetings or functions. If the group would rather hide some of their more controversial rites or "holy rituals," they will invite the potential member to an innocent get-together; a "family" picnic, or perhaps a class or lecture. The recruiting process for these cults is much slower, much more methodical—but the success rate is generally much higher, and the quality of recruit membership is greater.

For the persons being recruited, the passive cult is probably more dangerous because there is less pressure at the beginning to join, and therefore less of a chance that they will say no. Instead, their curiosity will be aroused and they will lead themselves into learning more about the group and eventually joining. Without the pressure, they also tend to feel that they are wholly in control of their own free will, and generally they commit themselves more totally to the group. These smaller cults can be found throughout our more rural communities.

Other cults recruit very actively. Some even hire public relations experts

---

Recruiting in itself is a very powerful form of mind control. First of all, for a cult member to be chosen to recruit is to bestow a very high honor on him or her. It is a sign of acceptance and reward.

Then, the actual practice of recruiting reinforces the cult's message in the mind of the recruiter through repetition of standard phrases and ideas, through the display of optimism and sincerity, and through the demonstration of conviction while trying to persuade others.

Finally, recruiters meet with a great deal of negative reaction, which gives them an opportunity to apply the defense techniques that they are taught. In others words, if someone tells them they are a cult, or are working for the devil, or are being guided down the wrong path or should be stopped, it reinforces in the recruiters' own minds that the group must be on the right track, that the outside world is evil and misguided, and that they are being persecuted. After all, no one said that "spreading the truth" would be easy. And imagine the joy and sense of accomplishment when a recruiter gets even one convert, and the strength it gives to his or her convictions.

to handle advertising, making their leaders well-known nationwide, and putting together public meetings or revivals to attract new members. Then it is up to the cult's "official" recruiters to net the new members.

Most cults fall between these two methods of recruiting, relying both on passive and active recruiting. And selecting the cult members to go to the college campuses, to the airline terminals, and to the youth clubs to recruit new members is very serious business.

Recruiters are chosen for their intelligence, their knowledge of the cult, their dedication to the group's cause, and probably more importantly, for their friendly nature, eternal optimism, and ability to charm and persuade.

Recruiters operate in many different ways. In some cults, they "preach the message." This is readily apparent among "revivalist Christian" cults such as Jim Jones' People's Temple cult. The object is to emphasize man's sinful nature and the need to repent and accept the true word as it is offered by the group and the group's savior.

Another cult may point out the social problems in the world and offer solutions. These types of cults were very prevalent in the sixties and seventies when there appeared to be many social injustices such as the Vietnam war, starvation, the threat of nuclear anihilation and the seemingly total lack of regard for the environment and life upon the planet. Though less prevalent, or at least less extremist, these groups are still active today.

Another group may espouse less government and more individualism. These groups promote less interference on such issues as abortion, where a child is to be schooled, how medicine is to be practiced, and others. These groups should not automatically be labelled "cults," but should only be regarded as cults when their activities become dangerous or harmful to children or to the general population. And it is usually left up to the courts to decide what is harmful.

Recruiters in the larger, harmful cults that practice mind control, generally approach potential new members with a broad smile and an appeal to family, to love of our fellow man, to hard work and clean living, to a need for discipline, and to rewards through conviction, perseverance and enlightenment. When using this approach, they are able to determine where a person's convictions or concerns lie, and they zero in. Is a person concerned about crime and getting actively involved in combatting it? Is a person concerned about his or her own salvation? Is a person interested in improving and better utilizing his or her talents in a particular area? The recruiter will promise solutions. Is a person looking for attention, for "family" love, for security and ease of emotional pain? The cult can provide that too!

One thing a recruiter is taught never to divulge is the truth about the cult. All the negatives including the strict discipline, the abuse, the real goal or beliefs of the cult are covered up. Recruiters feel it is okay to practice this deception because until people have been members of the cult for some time, they will not be able to understand or accept all of the teachings or practices of the cult. They have not yet attained the "level of enlightenment" necessary to understand all of the inner workings of the cult. They have not yet been "annointed" by the leader to receive the full doctrine of the cult. In reality, they have not yet been indoctrinated by mind control techniques to accept what the cult truly is all about.

Who is targeted for recruitment?

When analyzing who is targeted for membership into a cult, it is easier to determine who is **not** targeted. Cults usually ignore people who may be a liability in some way: the physically impaired who may require special attention and care, which uses up the group's time and money, and who have a limited ability to work for the group; the mentally unstable or mentally impaired; anyone with a serious health problem that requires expensive medical care; anyone who expresses disgust with the cult or the recruiters, especially if the person threatens to take action (by themselves or by contacting the law) against the group if they don't cease and desist; anyone who asks too many intelligent questions as if they were working with an anti-cult network to gain more information about the cult in an effort to undermine or expose their activities. Some cults are exclusively of one particular race (usually Caucasian) and exclude all other racial groups, or discriminate along ethnic lines; others may take whites and blacks but not Hispanics, for instance, or Asian-Americans but not native Asians. Most reject those who are openly homosexual.

Who does that leave? Probably about ninety percent of the population! And from this vast majority of the population, cults target new members.

People are targeted for recruitment by their vulnerabilities but more importantly, by what they have to offer the cult. Do they have beauty and charisma (they will attract other members and be good recruiters)? Do they have intelligence (they will become teachers and leaders within the goup)? Do they have a job skill (they will become the builders and money makers)? Do they have a profession (they will become part of the management team and/or will be able to give authenticity to the group)? Do they have money (obvious)?

In addition, religious cults look for people with strong religious backgrounds and convictions who, when fully indoctrinated, will provide additional religious conviction; and non-religious people who are "waiting to be saved" to provide testimonials.

Recruits can further be broken down into age groups:

Young adults, ages 18-25. — Young adults are especially attractive to cults because they fill many of the attributes listed above.

Young adults are usually more vulnerable than those over 25. They often are searching for truth and meaning in their lives. They are often dissatisfied with life as they have witnessed it so far. They are looking for someone to understand them, to nurture them, to believe in them and to protect them. If they are away from home for the first time, they are looking for friendship and an extended family.

Young adults also have a lot to offer. They have more strength to work hard and sleep little. They are more energetic, naively optimistic, and youthfully attractive, which makes them ideal candidates for recruiting. They are more easily shaped into the cult mold. They are more accepting of non-traditional behaviors or ideas. They are more open to discipline and guidance. They are more trusting of authority figures and are more willing to experiment with new ideas and new patterns of living.

Finally, young adults have great potential. Their leadership qualities, job skills, and professional abilities can all be nurtured and allowed to develop under the dogma of the cult. They are the true future of the cult.

The older generations (above 50). — The upper middle-aged and the elderly are also prime targets of cults, but for totally different reasons than young adults. First of all the elderly are vulnerable, not because they have left home, but because others in the home have left them, e.g., children have moved out, spouses have died, etc. This is the group most likely to suffer from losses such as a job (meaningful work as well as social interaction with co-workers); friends and relatives (through death or relocation); attention (children and others who now ignore them because they are old); and meaning in life (the previous institutions of which they were a part no longer meet their needs). In other words, the elderly are often lonely, and alone.

The older generations are also vulnerable to con artists, especially if during their lifetimes they have relied on others to make decisions or offer advice, and those others are now gone. Sometimes pride prevents the elderly from seeking advice or help from others. Activities of the elderly are often taken less seriously, or ignored altogether by others, especially children or family members, who normally would be in positions to offer words of caution. Sometimes the elderly are ignored, or not taken seriously, because they are seen as having lived a full life and therefore as being capable of recognizing potentially harmful groups or individuals.

Senior citizens who join cults often make stronger commitments and therefore are less apt to recognize or respond to the warning signs. They take a stand and stick with it.

The elderly who have had great achievements in their lives are often recruited for their stature and credibility. Those who have retired but continue to serve on boards of directors or are respected for their advice and opinion, especially in government or with large corporations, are sought out by cults for the influence they have. But generally, the elderly in this group are very difficult to recruit.

Finally, the elderly often have wealth or possessions (property) that the cult would like to have. The elderly sometimes are willing to trade wealth and possessions for love and attention, the promise of eternal salvation, protection, and the security that someone will always be there to take care of them if and when they need it. Unfortunately, the elderly often have the most to lose by joining a cult, and often are the first to lose it.

The middle-agers (26-49). — Generally, people over 25 but not yet 50, which includes so-called baby-boomers, have fewer vulnerabilities for cults to attack. They are out of school, or nearly so; they have been away from home and are often starting their own families; they usually have good jobs and do not lack for the basics (food, clothing, shelter); they have close friends and relatives; and they are politically and religiously associated with a group or groups that meet their needs. Quite often, people in this group are too busy to get involved in yet another activity that will only shorten their days and weeks.

In addition, people in the 26-49 age range, generally, are less controllable and susceptible to mind-control techniques such as isolation, sensory overload, group dynamics, changing of behavior and appearance, guilt, fear, and information control. Middle-agers, generally, are not looking to buy what cults are selling.

But there are exceptions. Not everyone in this age group has been successful in finding a mate. Many of those who have married are now divorced or are getting a divorce. And tragedies do occur that take away family, friends and loved ones. Jobs are sometimes lost and not easily replaced. People are transferred. Sometimes life does get boring, and people in this age group look for things new and different.

Rather than religious cults, people in this age group often are more vulnerable to political or social cults. They see their lives as being more threatened by social ills than by spiritual evils. They are more interested in improving man's lot on earth, rather than ensuring man's spiritual salvation. And they generally are more interested in groups or educational activities that will improve their job skills, strengthen their influence with their bosses or management, or improve the bottom lines for the businesses they own.

When couples in this age group are attracted to a cult, generally one spouse gets involved, then recruits the other spouse. If the second spouse refuses to join the group, it often creates an ever-widening chasm in the marriage, which ultimately ends in divorce or separation. If children are involved, the split can become quite painful and ugly, and the children can suffer emotional scars the rest of their lives.

When middle-agers get involved in religious cults, it is generally because they become disillusioned with traditional religions and seek enlightenment in New Age practices such as astrology, transcendental meditation and the occult. Although these practices do not belong exclusively to cults, and indeed, may be a part of, or at least be compatible with, some traditional religions, they nevertheless sometimes become the basis for cults. Satanic cults specifically have their roots in the occult.

Children (anyone under 18). — Children, obviously, are the most vulnerable group when it comes to manipulation and mind control, but for cults recruiting new members, children are usually protected because recruiters cannot get past the parents. What often happens is that instead of recruiting among this age group, cults will infiltrate schools and organizations that have direct contact with and influence children, conditioning them to be more open to cult ideas when they reach adulthood.

Perhaps the most heartbreaking circumstance of all is when a child is born into a dangerous cult. During his or her entire early life, the child is subject to the twisted mentality of cult parents and living in the cult environment, subject to the bizarre and often abusive beliefs and practices of the group.

Or, in cases where one parent joins a cult and the other does not, resulting in divorce or separation, the children are pulled in two directions. Obviously, under normal circumstances children face a difficult, often traumatic time when asked to choose between parents, but when one parent belongs to a cult, deception becomes a powerful tool, one that is next to impossible for a child to combat because of limited mental resources and life experience.

Indoctrination and Manipulation Within a Cult

During World War II, the Korean War, and more recently in Vietnam, brain-washing was used extensively on captured prisoners. These prisoners knew that their captors were trying to take control of the subconscious mind and reverse their inward thinking. This was done through sleep deprivation, physical and mental abuse, complete control of food and water, isolation, and constant torture and badgering.

Cults, too, use some brain-washing techniques. But there are dramatic differences. First of all, cult victims are cooperative; in fact, they don't know they are victims or prisoners because they willingly succumb. Secondly, the brain-washing is much more subtle, and eventually, more successful and more harmful mentally. The prisoner of war knows that the brain-washing will end in death or release, while the prisoner of a cult believes that enlightenment and salvation will be the reward. Finally, torture and abuse, if it is used at all by a cult, does not occur until indoctrination is complete and the victim is convinced the abuse is deserved.

It is important to know the differences between brain-washing, and mind control that uses brain-washing techniques, because many people, even the news media sometimes, perpetrate the misconception that cults use brain-washing to indoctrinate new members. Therefore, many mistakenly think that they are not vulnerable to cults, simply because they would be able to recognize when they are being indoctrinated because of obvious brain-washing techniques. In fact, it is this belief that we are invulnerable to brain-washing that makes each of us even more vulnerable to mind control. It makes us more vulnerable because we equate cults with brain-washing activities, and when we fail to recognize brain-washing techniques being used, we assume we are not dealing with a cult.

Methods of recruitment

What is a friend? A friend is someone who cares about you. A friend shares your likes and your dislikes, your dreams and your concerns. A friend provides support when you are down on your luck, hurting, or merely lonesome. A friend gives you hope and encouragement. A friend is trusting and loyal. And a friend accepts you as you are.

All our lives, we endeavor to surround ourselves with friends. And because friendships are such rare and fragile relationships, we value and protect them above most other concerns in our lives.

Cult members are friendly. They smile a lot, and seem to be very upbeat and positive. They are charismatic. They appear to be very self-assured. And they are attracted to you!

They are interested in you, what you do, what you like and dislike, how you live and work and play and worship, and what your favorite movies and television programs and types of music are. And chances are, they like what you like!

After connecting with you on a more casual level, your new "friends" will probe a little deeper. They will want to know what your needs and desires are, where you might be hurting or feeling a loss. They'll want to know your fears, your dissatisfactions and your disillusionments. And through all this, they will be understanding and supportive. They are on your side, they care about you, and they can be trusted because they are so sincere.

Finally, and quickly, they will seduce you, because they will have the answer to your problem, the formula for you to achieve your ambition, the secret to your happiness. The answers, of course, lie within the cult, and for you to reap the rewards you must join. But it is your choice to become a member of the group or not, your choice to leave if and when you decide to. You have absolutely nothing to lose and everything to gain. You have just been recruited into a cult.

While you are being recruited, something else is happening. Your new "friends" are sizing you up to see if you are really wanted by the group and what you have to offer. If it turns out you are not good cult material, your new "friends" will disappear from your life and you'll never know why.

If you are perceived to be good cult material, you will be cultivated and assessed for your strengths. You will be introduced to other members who are more likely to appeal to you, both mentally and physically. If you are a professional, you will be linked up with other professionals. If you are single and looking for companionship, you will be introduced to an attractive member of the opposite sex. If you are interested in success, you will meet members who are successful. Meanwhile, cult members will determine if you will best help the group through influence, money, ability to work hard, personality and physical appeal, organizational or motivational skills, or merely because of important contacts you may have. And if you don't know what is happening, you won't have a chance because cult members use mind control, which today has become a very sophisticated technique. And cult members are professionals at mind control. It is the heart and soul of the organization. It is what they know best.

Methods of mind control

To understand cult mind control, it is necessary first to understand the overall process, the result being that the recruit's reality is radically changed. So the cult will first break down the individual's current reality, or view of "how things are." Second, the cult will substitute the cult version of reality for the old reality. Finally, the cult reality is locked into place. All of this occurs, of course, without the awareness of the recruit that it is taking place.

Control of the environment

One of the first acts of control a cult uses is determining the environment. It may begin with meetings or seminars in a hotel meeting room (for larger groups) or a cult member's home (for smaller groups and individuals). Later the new member will be asked to attend retreats, lasting anywhere from a weekend to a couple of weeks, at a secluded setting, or, as in the case of the Branch Davidians, at the cult's own colony or compound. The ultimate goal, of course, is to have the new member move into a cult home or compound.

Almost all of a cult's mind control techniques are applied within the controlled setting. It keeps the new member from outside distractions, reinforces the community atmosphere, aids in the process of disorienting the person physiologically, and makes it more difficult for the new member to walk away from the proceedings.

Hypnosis

Hypnosis is a very broad and much-used technique for mind control. It is most often applied during lengthy lectures or sermons. It may also be effected through meditation and by taking part in rituals. It often occurs when a more experienced cult member talks one-on-one with a newer member.

The common element in all these activities is focused attention. As new members focus their attention on speakers, new information coming in, and in meditation, they gradually tune out the outside world. They allow their conscious, alert brains to close down to a comfortable, relaxed state. Researchers have found that in this almost euphoric state, people are very susceptible to new ideas, new concepts, to thoughts and suggestions. And they are less able to evaluate the validity or worth of those ideas.

Finally, hypnosis is a pleasant state. Therefore, it can be addictive. Cult members often find that they "ache" for another "fix" of the group leader's hypnotic talks.

Group dynamics

Group psychology plays a large part in shaping individual thoughts and actions. Cult leaders know the value of group dynamics, and try to fill an individual's time as much as possible with group activities. That is why most cults live in communes.

Generally, people want to conform—it's a lot easier! In a group setting, the individual can rely on the majority opinion being right. In a cult, the group setting allows only the group's interests to be heard. When individuals hear things that do not agree with their values, they reshape their values to match that of the group's.

Individuals are often asked to confess their past transgressions in a group setting. Then, to prevent group admonishment, they make atonement and are accepted more fully into the group. This is another technique for changing an individual's values and beliefs to match that of the group's.

Group settings also provide a convenient platform for sensory overload.

Sensory overload

Sensory overload is a method of depriving an individual of both mental and physical privacy. Without private time, individuals are unable to sort through the information coming in. Instead they are bombarded with lectures, group singing, meal preparation and other chores, and discussion groups until, exhausted, they climb into bed in their all-male or all-female dormitory room.

In lectures, the leader will talk rapidly, covering many subject areas non-stop. Followers are not allowed to interrupt, or to ask for explanations. They are expected to listen to the lectures, over and over, "until you begin to understand what I am saying. It will come to you." Of course the message does get to everyone eventually—through sensory overload.

Rewriting language

By introducing new meanings to words or phrases, a cult reinforces an individual's sense of belonging to the group, of sharing certain information that the outside world does not have. For instance, a "thinker" may be a term used for someone on the outside who is "messed up mentally." It becomes great fun for cult members, when out in public, to call someone by a cult name, "thinker," for instance. The other person considers it a compliment while the cult members chuckle in their knowledge that the word is derogatory. Cult members themselves do not want to be considered "thinkers," which encourages them to subconsciously shut off the thinking process without their even being aware of it.

Religious cults like to redefine language in the Bible. For instance, "sharing the love of God" may come to mean sleeping with the leader. The idea of "marriage" often takes on bizarre meanings within a cult.

Changing behavior and appearance

If you can change people's common behavior patterns, you can change their attitudes, beliefs and feelings. And if you change their appearance to conform to a group norm, you begin to change their attitudes, beliefs and feelings to match those of the group. The military effectively uses this technique in boot camp training; it is a recruit's introduction to the military way of life. Cults use the same technique, but it introduces the new member to the cult way of life and the cult belief structure (which is totally different from that of the military, of course).

Isolation

By isolating the cult from the outside world, cult leaders control the information members receive. Isolation also removes cult members from familiar environments that cause them to remember events, ideas and attitudes held before becoming cult members.

Isolation from the outside world also enables a cult leader to control reality, replacing the outside world view of reality (as reported by the news media and letters from relatives and friends) with the cult reality. That cult reality usually includes the picture that the outside world is misguided or evil, and ultimately, dangerous to the cult and to the members should they try to leave (leading to the stockpiling of arms in many cults).

Isolation also occurs within the cult. New members are split up (usually paired with a veteran member) to prevent them from swapping thoughts and ideas. And members rarely know all the things that are happening within the cult (such as some forms of abuse, sexual "privileges", or stockpiling weapons). They are told they will learn about other things in the cult when they have achieved a certain level of learning or have proven their dedication to the cult.

Childish behavior

Cult members are instructed to play-act as if they were children again, the reasoning being that they need to return to the innocence of childhood in order to shed the evil ways they learned in their former life. They are then given the cult's inspired learning and will be treated as adults only when they prove they have become adults (have accepted the cult indoctrination).

Cults also operate under the reward/punishment system. Good acts are rewarded; bad actions are punished. This reinforces the idea that, like children, cult members need guidance from their elders. Some cult leaders even ask members to call them "mother" or "father," thereby reinforcing the illusion of a parental authority figure.

The reward/punishment system also keeps members off balance. By never knowing for sure when they are going to be praised or punished, cult members learn to think less (about their actions) and perform mechanically. (Think of experiments in behavioral psychology where animals are taught to perform stunts or execute a maze through a process of rewards and punishment.)

Personal investment

The more time, money and effort people put into a project, the more they are likely to stick with it until they have attained their personal goals. The more time, money and effort people put into a cult, the more they become dependent upon the cult. Members that turn their life savings or their homes over to the cult, have none to return to should they decide to leave. It is often more convenient to stay, especially if they have alienated relatives and friends along the way. And for those who have invested a great deal of time and energy, it becomes more and more difficult to admit they were wrong and have wasted their investment. If and when cult members decide to leave a cult, they get nothing back!

Guilt

We all have done things or considered actions that make us less than proud. Cults encourage members to dredge up past actions or thoughts (usually in front of a group) for which they can be made to feel guilty. By admitting guilt, members acknowledge flaws in their identities, and submit to behavioral, emotional and/or mental changes that induce group conformity.

But in a cult, atonement for the past transgressions that caused the guilt is not enough. In a cult members are never forgiven. Rather, they are often reminded of past guilts in an effort to discredit their mental ability, further encouraging them to trust and rely on the thinking of the cult leader. Eventually, the members believe that the leader is thinking and acting in the best interest of the individual.

Cults also use guilt by association, reminding members that they once were members of a social group that engages in nuclear destruction of other peoples, that poisons the planet, that allows people to starve, etc.

Fear

Cults probably use fear to control their members more than any other single method of mind control. And it is used on several levels. Members fear making a mistake or thinking wrong thoughts for fear that they will incur the wrath of the leader, or will be seen less favorably. Members fear "spiritual" consequences of their thoughts and actions, such as being struck by lightening or having an accident (or even causing the holocaust!). And the fear of being wrong is powerful. What if you are wrong and the cult leader is right? Members fear losing the protection of the cult, or rather, what they perceive as "protection," including protection from the "evil influences" of the world outside the cult.

Fear is a very strong emotion that cults rely on heavily. But the ultimate fear, the fear of losing one's soul, is enough to cause many to choose to stay within a religious cult at all costs.

We/they mentality

In a cult, everything can be reduced to black or white, right or wrong, good or evil, weak or strong, us or them. And of course, the cult and its members have a monopoly on what is right, what is necessary to save the world or at least themselves. Therefore, all institutions, even other cults, are painted as being on the outside, without truth. Even individuals who are not members of the cult, including family and friends, are considered outside influences on the cult and its members and should be considered evil if they are not "saved."

Distortion of time

Cults live strictly in the here and now. A member's past prior to joining the cult is discounted because it is shaped by outside influences, not the cult's vision of reality. And there is no real future because the "end" is coming, and that may occur tonight or tomorrow. When the end does come, only those who are members in good standing with the cult will be saved; they will be rewarded for the sacrifices of today. By shrinking time, cults restrict members' thinking about what was in the past, or planning for what will be. Living for the cult, moment to moment, or one step at a time, is all that is necessary for salvation.

Information control

Many of the mind control techniques used by cults serve to limit the individual member's ability to think for themselves, to accurately see the whole picture. These techniques include filling a member's time, isolating a member from certain other individuals, and processing the information that the member is receiving. In addition, cults limit or even forbid such information resources as newspapers, radio and television, which may cause members to think about the reality outside the cult. When members do receive information from outside the cult (while buying supplies, working a job, etc.), that information is carefully reinterpreted by the cult leader to best serve the agenda of the cult.

Dietary control

Mental activity including thinking and perceiving are biological functions of the brain and may be altered biologically by the diet. A deficiency in Vitamin B_{12}, for instance, has been known to cause paranoia. B_{12} is not readily available in vegetable foods, and in fact is lost in people taking large amounts of vitamin C. B_{12} is found mainly in animal protein foods, and vegetarians often develop a B_{12} deficiency.

Low blood sugar can promote tension and anxiety, confusion and phobias. Low blood sugar, or hypoglycemia, can be brought about by fasting, or loading up the diet with refined carbohydrates.

A deficiency in animal protein and niacin can contribute to pellagra, a symptom of which is a psychosis resembling schizophrenia, and "swimmy-headedness" or mental confusion. (Sources for animal protein are red meat, fish, fowl, cheeses, milk and eggs. Vegetable protein including soy and nut protein is not fully equivalent to animal protein.)

In my research I've discovered that most cults are vegetarian, and many of them grow their own organic fruits and vegetables, as well as many herbs and spices. The Bible-based cults tell their members that to truly follow the teachings of the Bible, individuals must also follow dietary guidelines referenced in scriptures, and may interpret scriptures to mean eliminating specific foods such as caffeine, pork, unscaled fish, or other foods they determine to be harmful to the body. Many feel that all red meat is "unclean." Non-religious cults instruct their members that chemical additives in store-bought and restaurant-prepared foods are responsible for most, and sometimes all, of the diseases, especially cancer, of the industrialized world.

Herbal teas are much favored by cults because they are considered natural. But many herbal teas, taken in large amounts or continuously over a long period of time, can adversely affect the digestive system, the respiratory system, and the nervous system. Burdock root and seeds, for instance, can affect the nervous system resulting in anxiety, delirium, disorientation and seizures. And sassafrass, a very popular tea flavoring, was banned in 1960 by the FDA because it contains a potent cancer-causing agent, safrole.

Besides contributing to physical and mental ailments, restrictive diets serve cult leaders' purposes of mind control. The act of dieting enforces a code of strict obedience that helps change behavior patterns to match those of the leader. It also promotes conformity; a submission to group will over individual will. And finally, by controlling the diet, the cult leader reinforces the atmosphere of parent/child, with the parent (leader) knowing what is best for the child (follower).

Cults and the Law

What kind of protection from cults do you have under the law? Can you go to the police if you suspect that a family member is under the influence of cult mind control? What if you have evidence that a cult is involved in child abuse? If you were in a cult and turned over your life savings to them, can you get your money back? Is there any legal way to stop cult members from recruiting at airports, or schools, or at public gatherings? Aren't cults illegal?

The answer to all these questions is the same, "It depends."

Religious freedom and the right to assemble

To understand why it is so difficult to prosecute cults today, it is necessary to review our history and our national values to understand the attitudes concerning religious freedom and the right to assemble.

Just over 300 years ago, 19 people were killed and dozens more persecuted for witchcraft, beginning a period of repression and brutality in the name of religious "truth."

Less than 100 years later, our forefathers framed the constitution, adding the First Amendment, which guaranteed Americans the right to worship, to assemble peacefully, and to speak freely without restriction or repression.

During the decade of the 1950s, that Amendment was severely tested when the U.S. Congress, led by Senator Joseph McCarthy, sought to eradicate communism and its influences in America. Many innocent lives were destroyed on the weakest evidence of communist sympathy. Because the purge was so fanatic and out of control, civil liberties were widely violated, critical dissent was suppressed, absolute internal security measures were supported and national debate on major political issues was crushed. But it became apparent that America was fighting an imaginary demon, and in the process, very nearly destroyed a set of very basic human rights on which the nation was founded.

Then, in the late 1960s and early 1970s, the pendulum swung again and issues concerning protection under First Amendment rights were tested. Did people have the right to protest a war they considered unjust? Or question authority? Or demonstrate a set of values that clearly opposed "the norm?" Individual rights were pushed to the opposite extreme.

We continue to struggle with the question of human rights today, even to the extent that it often becomes unclear who is the persecutor and who is the victim. Who possesses what rights, and whose rights are being protected?

Our courts and law enforcement agencies today are tackling these very difficult questions, and it often appears, perhaps out of guilt over our past persecution of the innocent, that our judges are reluctant to restrict the activities of groups, especially when charges are built on suspicion and heresay. Proof must be established, and in cases dealing with cult activities, that proof is often hidden in deception.

Laws can work for or against cults

It is illegal to discriminate against people simply because they ascribe to different beliefs. Cults know that principle quite well, and in fact, base their entire existence on adherence to a set of beliefs. Religious cults go even further, hiding behind the First Amendment's guaranteed freedoms regarding religion. And they are able to abuse the legal system in the name of religion. However, the First Amendment does not protect religious leaders and their followers from prosecution and conviction when they violate criminal laws. Therefore, it is necessary, not to attempt to determine the illegality of a cult or bring charges against a cult based on its mere existence (in an attempt to destroy or disband a cult), but to attack specific illegal activities for which a cult may be guilty. Those suspected crimes include, but are not limited to, the following areas:

Mind control. — For many years, the law did not recognize that mind control existed. Court decisions were based on the belief that everyone is endowed with the right to freely choose a belief system, and if that belief system shapes and changes the person's thoughts, feelings and actions, it is not a product of mind control or coercion, but the result of a person's right to choose.

Eventually, courts began to realize that some destructive cults use fraud and deception in their recruiting and indoctrination of new members, reducing their capacity for informed consent, and leading to a "blind faith." This faith is further reinforced by techniques that we now recognize as mind controlling. Therefore, it is now possible to build a case against a cult leader or cult followers based on "persuasive coercion."

Child custody. — When hearing child custody cases, courts invariably look at environments and how they affect "the best interests of the child." If one parent is an active cult member and requests custody of a child, the court will determine the authoritarian structure of the cult and the ways the cult controls both the parent and the child. It will also evaluate the rules, practices and relationships within the cult to which the child would be exposed, with

36

regard to the formative effect they may have on the child's development. This includes the daily routine of cult life to determine how and with whom the child spends time, the kinds of discipline and education, the extent and nature of parental interaction with the child, and an analysis of the relative fitness of the parent emotionally, financially and otherwise. If child custody is to be denied to the parent or parents active in a cult, it must be proven that the cult environment is not in the best interests of the child.

If a child has entered a cult of his/her own free will, parents may regain custody through the legal process since, in general, the law gives parents the legal right to control the child's education and upbringing, including religious training.

Conservatorship. — In cases where adults wish to "free" a son or daughter from a cult, where the child has reached the age of majority (as defined by the statutes of the state in which the legal action is taken, usually between sixteen and eighteen), action may be taken through the filing of a conservatorship. In this case, it must be proven to the satisfaction of the court that the adult-child is suffering from a recognized medical (which may include psychiatric) condition, is unable to care for him or herself, and is not getting proper medical attention while in the cult.

It may be very difficult to gain legal custody through a conservatorship. The cult invariably will claim religious status; therefore, claims based on symptoms or harms caused by cult membership (a personal opinion) may be thrown out based on First Amendment protections given to religious organizations. Also, it may be impossible to gain access to the adult-child cult-member long enough for expert observation and health evaluation. Finally, courts may be reluctant to grant conservatorships over adult children who object, choosing to remain with the cult.

(Sadly, parents, friends, and often former cult members who have been blocked by the court system from "freeing" an individual from a cult have resorted to kidnapping, and sometimes "deprogramming," in an honest effort to restore the victim's mental and physical health. Such action often ends in a lawsuit being filed—and won!—by the cult and the victim against the parents.)

Criminal offenses. — While cults often hide behind the First Amendment, religious cult leaders and their followers are not protected if they violate criminal laws. Therefore, cult members may be convicted of filing false income tax returns, drug possession and dealing, conspiracy to obstruct justice, theft or burglary, fraud, possession of illegal weapons, pornography, violating immigration laws, physical abuse, and property destruction. Protecting the health, safety and welfare of the citizenry will frequently outweigh the need to protect a religious practice.

For instance, in the course of establishing practices within a religious cult, a cult leader may decide (through divine inspiration, of course) that he may have sexual intercourse with any other member of the cult as part of its religious practices. If someone brings charges against the cult because of this practice, the cult leader will be asked in court whether or not it is part of their religious practice for the leader to engage in extra-marital sexual relations with cult members. If the answer is no, then the court can rule that this practice is illegal. If the answer is yes, then this practice must be revealed to anyone being recruited or indoctrinated into the cult, or the cult would be held liable for fraud. In either case, it puts the cult leader in a difficult position, either with the courts or with his members.

Issues such as recovery of money freely given to a cult may be successfully defended if fraud is clearly proven.

Cult members may be prevented from recruiting at airports, schools or institutions which are considered private property if the property owners choose to restrict their activities. However, cults cannot be deprived of their constitutional rights to free speech on public property, and, therefore, can actively recruit on most high school and college campuses, and at public institutions, as long as they do not resort to harassment. Their activity can be curtailed, and in some cases stopped, if they are asked to identify themselves and their organizations and observe procedures of open expression (such as admitting anti-cult protesters to their meetings).

Your local police and protection

Police departments vary in size according to the density of the population. And the larger the police department, the greater the likelihood that it will have a unit that specializes in cult activities. But all police departments will respond in some manner to complaints or charges made by a citizen against cult activity that is perceived to be illegal or life-threatening. Obviously, if a crime has been committed such as a burglary, a beating or disturbing the peace, the police will respond and apprehend the individual or individuals committing the crime.

But what happens in most cases concerning cults is that there is only a suspicion that a crime has been committed, or there is suspected criminal intent. Without physical evidence or proof that a crime has been committed, police can do little more than investigate the complaint. Never will a police department attempt to infiltrate a suspected cult, nor will it attempt to "deprogram" a cult member at someone else's, usually a family member's, request.

It is important to remember that although law enforcement agencies can do little about controlling "legitimate" cult activities, all activities involving a known or suspected cult should be reported. Police departments keep files on organizations involved in questionable practices. Each reported incident sends up another red flag. Eventually, a suspected cult may engage in an illegal activity, at which time the police may step in and make arrests. The citizen reports, which may have been collected over several years' time, will be used as evidence to build the case against the cult.

The kinds of criminal activity most likely to be associated with a cult are possession and/or distribution of narcotics (as a means to finance their operation), and the possession of illegal weapons (unlicensed automatic or illegally modified firearms).

The types of cults that give police the greatest concern are the subversive cults that have ties to known terrorist organizations (usually Eastern religious groups), and satanic cults, which are more difficult to identify and penetrate.

Meanwhile, cults attempt to be model citizens, at least outwardly. Any criminal activity is shrouded in secrecy. The group maintains a tight-knit, quiet, isolated existence. And for most of them, the child abuse, the mind control, the deception and the fraud are never revealed until someone (usually from within the cult) dares to blow the whistle.

Protecting Yourself from Cults

If you have read this book to this point, you have come a long way in gaining the best protection there is against cults—knowledge. The more you know about cults and how they operate, the more protection you will have.

Earlier I mentioned that intelligence was no protection from cults. That is true. There is a difference between intelligence and knowledge. You can be very smart, but if you aren't aware of the ways that cults manipulate you and gain control of your reasoning powers, you may as well throw all your intelligence out the window. In fact, if you've come under the influence of a cult, your very intelligence will work against you because you will have a false sense of security that you will be able to recognize whether or not the group is telling you the truth. Intelligence doesn't tell you when you've lost your reasoning power.

How to recognize if you are being recruited

If you are approached to join or learn more about a group, or are asked to attend a lecture or seminar that promises to enhance your life in some way, there are a few questions you can ask up front. Remember, if it is a cult, especially a harmful cult, you will be lied to, so pay special attention to the facial expressions and body language of the suspected recruiter.

What is the name of your group? — Legitimate organizations will have a name and will tell you. Illegitimate organizations will rarely have a name, or the recruiter will tell you they are not affiliated with an organization, or will tell you a purpose of the group but not the name, or will give a false name. How the individual responds should give you clues as to his/her purpose.

What organization is sponsoring the lecture/seminar? — This is especially important if you are attending school and the lecture or seminar seems to be school related. Don't assume—ask if it is a school-sanctioned activity. (It is not enough that the lecture or seminar is given by a school instructor or recommended by an instructor.) But even if the group has the sponsorship or recognition by a school or reputable organization, do not assume it is right for you. The group still could be masking their true identity.

What is the agenda? — If the purpose of the meeting or seminar is for recruiting new members, the agenda will be carefully hidden in generalities. Be especially inquisitive if the invitation is for a weekend get-away. How

41

will your time be filled? Who are the speakers? What are the topics? What is the purpose? Why are you being asked and why is it so reasonable or free?

How are you involved in the group and how long have you known them? — The answer to this question could be very revealing. Trust your instincts as to whether the individual is honest and open or is hiding something. If you are being approached by friends, ask how they got involved in the group. If it appears that they had a need fulfilled "beyond all expectations," (the too-good-to-be-true feeling), it meets the pattern that dangerous, mind-controlling cults fit.

You may be getting the feeling that these questions border on paranoia. After all, shouldn't we be open to new friends, new opportunities for growth and understanding, new avenues of relaxation and enjoyment? Of course. But we can do all of that and still be careful, and if all the questions are answered to our satisfaction, we can be more confident about the organization and taking the next step, attending the lecture, meeting, or even a weekend retreat.

Recognizing a cult from the inside

The second step to protecting yourself from becoming involved in a dangerous cult is to be aware. If you've accepted an invitation to attend a group function, be it a meeting or lecture, a "family" picnic, or a weekend retreat, you'll likely meet the friendliest people you've ever met in your life. They will instantly like you and will be caring, consoling and understanding, cheerful and self-assured. Enjoy yourself and your new-found friendships, but don't let your guard down at this critical stage. Be aware.

The general conversation. — What kinds of questions are you being asked? In their friendliness, are others getting you to reveal your innermost thoughts and feelings? Do you suddenly find you are comfortable revealing to them an innermost problem or concern, a fear or a wish? Do they tell you they understand and that the group was just meant for someone like you? Be aware.

Isolation. — When talking with people in the group, do they separate you from any friends who may have come with you? Do they separate you from anyone else who is being recruited and who appears to be too inquisitive? Are they controlling your surroundings? Be aware.

Criticism. — Do any of the people in the group criticize, or encourage you to criticize your family or other religions or organizations? Do they make you feel guilty about your past in any way? Be aware.

Pressure. — Are you pressured to be a part of the group "because everyone

42

else is doing it?" Are you pressured to join now, "while the iron is hot?" Is it true that you may never have a chance like this again? Be aware.

Easy solutions. — Does the group have simple answers to complex problems, an easy fix? Does the group have solutions to all your problems? Be aware.

Vagueness. — Does the group continue to be vague about their true agenda, the way they operate, what happens at other group meetings, or what they will expect of you once you have joined? Be aware.

In addition to being aware of the group, also be aware of yourself. If you find yourself interested in a particular group, it is a good time to re-evaluate yourself to find out why you are interested.

Are you lonely? — We all get lonely sometimes, especially when events in our lives separate us from friends or relatives or a secure environment. Ask yourself what part this new group may have in your life and if your need for the group goes beyond your need for friendship and understanding. It may be better to look somewhere else for a cure for your loneliness.

Are you suffering a loss? — Losses in our lives make us more vulnerable to cults. Has there been a sudden illness, accident or death near you? Have you recently lost your job or moved to a new location? Have you been a victim of a crime, divorce or separation, or natural disaster such as a flood or fire? Be aware of the losses in your life and how they may be affecting you.

Are you seeking? — You may be looking for spiritual guidance or fulfillment, or a better world order, or personal mastery in some area, or enlightenment on some mystery of life such as astrology or the psychic. Does this group promise to give you answers? What is the price you must pay to get those answers?

Do you feel unimportant? — We all get a certain satisfaction out of praise from others. But is that praise legitimate? In the beginning, cults feed the needs of their new members to feel wanted, needed and important. They build up egos and self-esteem. They make their new members feel self-assured and even powerful. But in a very short time, members are made to feel like dependent children. And how is your ego?

Do you want security? — It's always nice to have someone to rely on to take care of all our insecurities, from making tough choices in our lives to providing love, food and shelter. How secure are you, and what promises would be difficult for you to turn down?

Do you suffer from low self-esteem? — We all have feelings about ourselves physically, socially, emotionally and intellectually. We develop opinions about our own abilities and skills. When we don't feel comfortable with those feelings and opinions, we often look to others and determine our self-worth by their opinions, making us extremely susceptible to a cult.

Cults need you

Always remember that cults are not interested in helping you, but in helping themselves. And nearly all their membership comes through recruitment. You are important to them. They want your time, your mind and your money. They want control of your life. Don't give it away to anyone. Think for yourself. It is your best protection against cults.

Protecting Others from Cults

What would you do if a son or daughter told you they were moving into a commune? Or what if a parent no longer wrote to you, or suddenly got an unlisted phone and refused to give you the number? Should you suspect that they have become members in a destructive cult? How would you know for sure? Should you intervene? How?

These are not easy questions to answer. But here are a few guidelines to get you started.

Recognizing cult involvement

We all go through changes in our lives, especially during our teen and early adult years. With these changes often come personality changes. Do you remember how you acted when you first fell in love? Changes in a person's appearance or behavior could result from a number of things besides cult involvement. With that in mind, here is a list of clues that might indicate a friend or family member is involved in a cult.

Personality change. — A sudden change from general happiness to total seriousness; changing from interest in family activities to isolation; dropping memberships in clubs and organizations, especially religious organizations; dropping old friends for new; becoming secretive.

Goal change. — Suddenly quitting a job or leaving school; sudden poor performance in school work and/or changing course of study; dropping athletics or band or the drama club because "they no longer mean anything"; suddenly becoming environmentally conscious or politically involved or religious; spending all their free time with "a study group."

Spending money. — Suddenly transferring funds, selling assets or possessions, and emptying bank accounts for no obvious reason; raising funds for a "special" organization.

Breaking ties. — Suddenly breaking all ties with family; refusing to write letters or take phone calls; suddenly relocating and leaving no forwarding address or even destination. Sometimes new cult members break ties with family, but keep in touch with one friend, and it is that friend who alerts families to what is happening in the life (and head) of the cult member.

Other warning signs. — Involvement in a satanic cult is often manifested by additional activities including changes in eating and sleeping patterns; beginning or increased alcohol or drug use; serious misbehavior such as graffiti, vandalism, or cruelty to animals; profanity; an obsession with books, movies, videos and records that have themes of violence, rape, death and demonism; a sudden change in appearance with particular attention to colors, especially black; and a sudden interest in satanic symbols.

Should you get involved?

Should you get involved when you notice the very first signs that a family member might be involved with a cult? Or should you wait to see if things change back to normal, in case it is "just a stage they are going through?" If you wait, could it become too late? Again, these are tough questions to answer, but there are things you can do to help you decide.

Keep communication lines open. — If a family member is involved in a cult, and if you are still communicating, keep those communication lines open at all costs—it may be your loved one's only link to reality. And it is probably just a matter of time before it is lost. Meanwhile, always stay calm and supportive. Listen to the cult member's point of view. Ask questions, but don't try to change their opinions or admonish them in any way. Remind them of what you know to be some of their fondest memories, but never bring up unpleasant experiences. Find out what they believe and why. Show your emotions (they will be able to detect insincerity) but do so calmly and do not accuse them of making you sad or angry. Allow them to disagree with you. Plant "seeds" of doubt in their new beliefs, but at the same time, respect their right to think differently from you. Encourage them to keep you informed about what they are doing and where they are. And most importantly, let them know that you love and respect them.

Contact resources. — Initiate contact with the cult awareness organizations in the appendix of this book and ask for information and guidance. Not all resources will have all the answers for you; therefore, it is recommended that you contact as many as you can and determine later which ones best fit your needs. Also remember that all cult awareness organizations do not have all the information about all cults. Unless you are inquiring about a well-established cult, the resource organizations will ask for your help in building a profile on the suspected cult. But in the meantime, they can all give you valuable advice in how to proceed with your involvement.

Go to the library. — Read all you can about cults and how they operate. Start with the bibliography at the back of this book. Ask the library for any new books published on the subject of cults. Much information is also available now on videotape or computer disk. Ask the library reference desk how you go about finding television special reports, or write directly to the major networks.

Go to the police. — Report what you know about the cult. Ask if any other reports have been filed. If the cult activity is in another city, contact your own police department and ask them to keep you informed of any developments they may become aware of.

Call the newspaper. — Newspapers in the city where the cult is located often have files of information related to the cult and are more than happy to share that information. But they will also ask you for information that will help them in their news gathering. Where appropriate, ask to speak to the specific reporter assigned to the story. If the newspaper has no information on a suspected cult, ask to stay in touch with the newspaper. When talking to the news media, never make unsubstantiated claims, and be prepared to give sources for all your information.

Contact ex-cult members. — Ex-cult members can be difficult to find, and usually will be found through the cult awareness organizations. If it is the organization's policy not to release names and addresses, ask them to forward your request to the former member(s). Former members will be extremely helpful in learning more about the cult, and will be extremely valuable in helping free your family member.

Contact the District Attorney. — The District Attorney's office in the cult's hometown may be able to provide you with information that you can't get from other sources.

Federal Bureau of Investigation. — The FBI monitors many cults and cult activities. Although they may be reluctant to talk to you, it would be worth trying. They probably will have more questions for you than you do for them, but the contact could be very important and helpful.

Social and welfare agencies. — This is a much-overlooked potential resource. They may be aware of child abuse, welfare or social security payment abuses, or immigration problems associated with a cult or a potential cult.

Never give up! Be patient, and expect to be involved for a very long time. If you don't feel you have the patience or energy to research a cult properly, hire someone (reputable) to do it for you.

Don'ts for family members

Don't send money. — If you suspect a family member is involved in a cult, they will probably ask you for money. Instead of money, ask if you can help them by sending non-cash items such as clothing, non-refundable airline tickets or books. If they want to settle an account, ask them to send you the bill. If you are convinced the bill is legitimate (for tuition, books, rent, etc.), and you feel the need is real, pay the bill directly.

Don't give up. — Remember that the one thing that cannot be taken away through mind control is a person's past. That includes all the love, the training, the genes and the home environment that you provided. Those things may seem to be hidden, but more often than not, they are the single fragile thread of hope in getting your loved one back. Keep trying!

Don't alienate yourself. — Whether you are talking to your family member who is in a cult, another cult member, or the cult leader, never make yourself the "heavy" by down-grading the cult or its leader. It will only alienate you and put more of a wedge between you and your loved one. Always maintain a positive attitude and relationship.

Don't talk theology. — Or politics, or sociology, or business (depending on the type of cult). The cult has already convinced your loved one that you are the primary source of their evil past. So you don't stand a chance arguing the point. Instead, listen to their views, even question their views, but never discount them. You will only be making it more difficult to reverse their thinking.

Don't face the problem alone. — Many families throughout the world have gone through what you are experiencing right now. Search them out and start meeting together. Pull together or join a support group to share your frustrations, your joys, your trials and your progress. It will help more in the healing process than you can possibly fully understand.

Don't try to infiltrate the cult. — Never think you can infiltrate by joining the cult, then trying to persuade your loved one to get out. You are dealing with experts in mind control. Their techniques are so subtle and persuasive, you can easily get caught up in their thinking and forget the mission you were on. Besides, if you are found out by the cult, you will be exposed and used as an example to the rest of the group, further alienating your loved one.

Don't show your hand. — If you have contact with other members, or suspected members, in the cult, or with the cult leader, never give them information about your cult investigation activities, no matter how much you trust them. The information will be used against you and could cause harm to your loved one.

Don't use propaganda. — Cult members have been warned that family members will try to get them to leave the cult by sending newspaper or magazine articles, television or radio tapes, or books written about their group. These things will only serve to remind them that the "evil in the outside world" is trying to harm them.

Don't blame yourself. — You must protect you own mental health. The quickest way to destroy it is to blame yourself.

Do's for family members

Keep communication lines open. — Answer and encourage all correspondence (phone calls, letters, personal contact) from your family member with a loving, sincere, non-critical attitude. Be consistent and show you really care.

Keep a record. — Record all names, addresses and phone numbers of persons known to be associated with your family member's cult, and activities outside the cult. Also make it a habit to get the names and phone numbers of anyone contacting you concerning information about your loved one or the cult. You may want to contact those people later when you have a better understanding of the situation. Accurate documentation also may be vital in reconstructing events or identifying individuals at a later time.

Maintain contact. — Regularly keep in touch with law enforcement agencies, cult awareness organizations and other resources you have cultivated during the course of your research. You will be surprised when and from where you could receive a bit of information that will help you in your quest. If you should lose contact with your loved one, and in turn move to another city, make sure your loved one will be able to find you through other relatives or organizations should he/she leave the cult and want to return home.

Inside the Branch Davidians

When self-appointed prophet David Koresh led his followers to a stand-off with federal agents in Waco, Texas in 1993, a nation watched in disbelief. How far would 85 people go to defend their seemingly insane "savior," their fabricated belief structure, and a hollow "message of salvation?"

Fifty-one days later we learned the incredible answer. On Monday, April 19, 1993, in a spectacular fireburst, the Waco compound exploded killing David Koresh and his 85 followers, including 17 children.

As I witnessed the brilliant and thunderous explosions on television with my son Robert, a large part of me seemed to be taken away with the smoke. I felt I had known David Koresh from the many conversations we had on the phone. I had read letters my son shared with me from Jimmy Riddle and others who died in the fire. I thought about the 17 children, who in their innocence, were offered no choice but to die. How could it happen? I asked my son for explanations.

"Did you **really** believe David Koresh was Jesus Christ?" I asked.

"Yes."

"Do you mean that if you had not been sent home when you were, that you would have followed David Koresh and the others into death?"

My son stared at me with his large, determined brown eyes. "I would have killed for him. I would have died for him. I didn't want to leave, and if I hadn't been sent home, I would have been reincarnated with him now."

I couldn't understand, but I believed my son. And as I watched the images on television settle to ashes, I vowed to learn about the incredible power that cults and cult leaders have over their followers. I asked Robert to help me understand.

Pomona, California, the spring of 1989

When Robert arrived in California, his head was filled with great expectations. With three years of military service behind him and a technical degree in hand, he had his first job since graduating as an avionics technician. He shared a mobile home with two others, 1200 miles away from family and friends. He was wide-eyed, ambitious and hopeful. I could tell by his letters and phone calls that he was applying the same dedication on the job that he had put into his studies. He was determined to learn, to understand,

and to apply his talents.

But life does not unfold with the promise and predictability of a textbook. After six months, Robert's company began downsizing and he was laid off. Other aviation firms where he applied for work were going through the same economic throes. Meanwhile, after his roommates stole many of his personal effects, he turned to temporary housing at a shelter provided by the church he was attending.

One afternoon, while Robert was doing his laundry, Jimmy Riddle happened into the same laundromat and the two friends renewed their camaraderie. Jimmy was still working as a custodian at the avionics firm adjacent to Robert's former employer. Robert enjoyed Jimmy's bright banter, his understanding of Robert's situation and his genuine warmth and concern. Jimmy had always impressed him by his cheerfulness and dedication on the job, and now Jimmy reached out his hand in aid.

Robert still felt a bit envious of Jimmy, remembering an earlier conversation in which Jimmy had mentioned planning to take some vacation time to go on a religious retreat in Texas. "People from all over the world will be there to study the Bible," Jimmy said. Robert asked about the retreat. Sensing that Robert might be interested in the religious group, Jimmy invited him to his house to meet other members of his "adopted family."

At the house, Robert was introduced to Steve Schneider, a man in his middle thirties, blond, and with a very friendly personality that immediately instills respect and trust. Steve explained to Robert that the Bible was now harmonized, that the Old and New Testaments were now in agreement. Intrigued by this possibility, Robert wanted to learn more.

Over the next few weeks, Robert accepted several invitations to return to the "family" home to discuss the Bible. On his second visit, he was instructed by Sherry Jewell, a former school teacher who told stories from the Bible in a very understandable, mesmerizing manner. She, too, was very open and friendly, and Robert immediately felt a rapport with her and her attractive daughter.

On his third visit, Robert met a small group of people who sat in a circle in the living room of the stone house, listening to the various speakers give interpretations of lessons from the Bible.

On his fourth visit, Robert met David Koresh (at that time he was still known as Vernon Howell), who talked to him one-on-one about the Bible. David would ask Robert to quote anything he wanted from the Bible. Robert would open his book and begin reading when David would interrupt him, finishing the Bible verses from memory, and give his interpretation. Robert was very impressed by the man's knowledge and ease with the teachings of the Bible.

Needing to find a more permanent place to stay, and feeling a kinship with this very special group of people who shared his love of the Bible, Robert asked if they had room for him to stay at the house. David Koresh seemed taken by surprise and told Robert that he wasn't running a boarding house. Robert laughed and reiterated his desire to be a part of the group. David told him that he must accept his teachings, Robert agreed, and the group welcomed him into their home.

Conditions were crowded at the house. Robert took his sleeping bag, backpack, and a small metal locker, and camped out on the dirt floor of the musty, drafty garage behind the house. It was the men's dormitory where, over the next several weeks, as many as twenty men at a time were resident. Jimmy Riddle slept in the camper shell of his pickup truck, parked next to the garage. The women made accommodations in the house. David Koresh, when he was in town, stayed in the house.

Because of the large number of people living so closely together, strict rules and regulations were followed. Individuals were allotted time segments in which to use bathroom facilities, especially during the rush hours in the morning, but there never seemed to be any problems or conflicts.

Occupants were assigned chores, which insured that the bathroom, as well as the rest of the house, was always clean. Meals were prepared and the dishes were washed. It was, indeed, one very large, happy and well-organized family. Robert felt fortunate to be accepted by this warm and very caring group of people.

Soon Robert found a job at another avionics firm and was able to contribute his share to the upkeep of the house and for his food. But working became secondary. Learning and understanding the teachings of David Koresh gradually consumed Robert's interest, as it had with those he lived with.

There was a schedule for everything except for David's teachings. When inspiration touched him, David would assemble everyone in the living room for a Bible session. Sometimes the sessions would last a few minutes, sometimes they would go on for hours. They could occur during the day, which required that everyone not away at work drop the chores they were doing to listen to him; they could occur in the middle of the night, at which time everyone would be awakened to attend the session.

At all times, David Koresh was in total control. He was always informal, sometimes standing and delivering a dramatic story from the Bible, sometimes sitting on the floor and playing with his feet or eating a sandwich and quoting from the Bible and giving his interpretation. Sometimes he strummed his guitar, putting together a special message into the form of a song. Always, he held everyone's attention and spoke with a divine wisdom and knowledge. Using his own words, everyone considered him the "Lamb of Revelation." Robert knew he was in the privileged company of someone special.

Robert knew that he was special too. Soon after his arrival at the house, David Koresh singled Robert out to accompany him on a spiritual mission. Robert cleaned up and shaved while David had his hair braided by Sherry Jewell. David Koresh got out the motorcycle, Robert climbed aboard behind him and the two were off on their mission.

They called on a young couple who were members of the Seventh Day Adventist church, the denomination David preferred to recruit from. With Robert sitting to his right and the couple seated directly across from him, David proceeded to read from the Bible and give his interpretation. The young couple seemed genuinely interested, following in their own well-marked Bible, but after two hours Robert began to nod off. David admonished him for not being ready to accept his teachings and they left shortly after.

Robert recalls that after they returned to the house, everyone was disappointed for the young couple. They had chosen not to accept David's teachings and the group expressed concern for their souls being lost. And it was then that Robert learned that his "job" during the recruiting mission was to act enthusiastic in an effort to stir an emotional positive reaction from the couple. He was never asked to go on another mission.

For two weeks, Robert went to work, did his chores at the house, and listened to David Koresh preach, but no matter how hard he tried, he never totally grasped the message or understood the points David was trying to make. He was always persuaded to take his time, to keep an open mind, to concentrate on David's words, and that eventually it would all come together for him "when the time is right."

Meanwhile, David would hold review sessions in which he sped through lesson after lesson, exhilirating everyone. No one was allowed to interrupt him with questions. If the meaning wasn't clear, it would become clear later. "Take it by faith now; you'll see later. Just concentrate and listen. Soon enough you will learn," David would say. Determined to get the message, Robert spent all his free time reviewing phrases and concentrating on David's words. At night he would fall asleep, concentrating on receiving the light.

Suddenly, one day it happened. It all became clear to Robert. David had been reading from the Book of Revelations about a man named Faithful and True who was riding a white horse. The man's eyes were as a flame of fire and on his head were many crowns. Koresh told his followers that that man was holding up a Bible in his right hand and his name was Christ. He then asked them to close their eyes and follow along with the vision that he, David, had, and he continued to describe Christ on the white horse. Then he asked them to open their eyes.

"That describes me, doesn't it?" David asked. "I am the man riding that white horse and I'm holding the Bible in my right hand. You believe it, don't you? You do see it with your own eyes, don't you?"

And Robert saw. He understood the true meaning of the messages. He was feeling exhilarated and true acceptance into the group, for finally he understood what everyone else knew—David Koresh was Jesus Christ! The revelation was incredibly powerful.

Life inside the cult

For the next several weeks, Robert fell into the routine of work, chores, instruction and sleep. But life was different now because he had a strong sense of direction and meaning. He was able to share his new purpose on earth with teachers, engineers, lawyers, nurses, former pastors, construction workers and janitors, all followers of David Koresh. They ranged in age from the teens to the sixties, making it a multi-generational family. But all was not well in paradise.

David Koresh was always the final authority in every matter, and because of his spiritual nature, was never questioned publicly. But following in his footsteps was very difficult. David would treat his followers like small children, freely giving reprimands much like an insensitive parent, "You know better than that, now don't you? What's going on in your head? What do you have for brains, spaghetti?" Inside, his followers cowered.

But the study sessions continued, sometimes lasting as many as eighteen hours without stop, yet no one left or complained. Literally, they were under his spell, anticipating and accepting every word as if in a state of hypnotic acceptance. During those times between lectures, most cult members felt an addictive need for another "fix" of inspirational teaching.

But was this a cult? Robert remembers many occasions where members joked and laughed at the mere suggestion. This immediately threw suspicion off and he dismissed his own concerns as foolish. Besides, there were no obvious signs of cult activity. For instance, he was not asked to give all his money and possessions to the group (although later he could not recall what he did with his paychecks, or whether or not he even had a bank account. This part of his life in the cult seemed to be erased, in his words, "because money and material things were unimportant to us.")

Also, members were free to leave the group, and many did. But those who stayed became stronger and stronger in their convictions.

David Koresh developed much of his mind control over his followers by establishing a strict dietary regimen. By quoting and interpreting scriptures, he was able to convince his followers that certain foods were unclean, such as red meats (especially pork) and foods commercially prepared with chemicals and additives. So the Branch Davidian diet was deficient in animal proteins and high in carbohydrates.

Forbidden were such foods as pork, shrimp, chocolate, coffee, regular tea, cakes and sodas. Rarely did they have beef or any animal products. Instead, meals were prepared with fresh fruits, limited amounts of vegetables, poultry and breads. Turkey hot dogs were a common favorite. Popcorn was served regularly, especially after long study sessions. Sometimes it was the only food available on a given day. Other times, just popcorn and fruit.

But to keep his followers off balance and dependent on his "wisdom," David Koresh added other food restrictions. Liquids, including water, were not allowed at meals. And certain foods could not be eaten together. For instance, oranges could be eaten with grapes but not with raisins. Fruit could not be eaten with vegetables unless the vegetable was freshly cooked corn or the fruits were lemons, pineapples or avocados. Apples could be eaten with vegetables if they were stewed first, as Koresh believed that the chemistry of the apple changed when cooked.

Men were sometimes allowed to drink beer, but only certain brands, and no more than two spaced one hour apart.

Vitamins and dietary supplements were not allowed.

Certain members were assigned the chore of preparing the food. They even prepared sack lunches for those who worked regular jobs. Take-out lunches usually included fruit and turkey hot dogs or a vegetable patty. One member blended the tea from herbs and tea leaves kept in plastic bags in the kitchen.

David Koresh did not follow his own dietary regimen, however. He was put on this earth, he would explain, to experience and suffer all the sins of the world (which included the sin of eating unhealthy foods) so that when he stood in judgment of sinners on Judgment Day, he would have "experience of all sin and degradation on earth." Consequently, he would sometimes savor a large bowl of ice cream in front of a group of followers, telling them to give thanks to him for taking on their sins while they remained pure and clean.

Life in the Branch Davidian house was without outside influence. Radios, television, newspapers and magazines were forbidden (except for David

Koresh, of course). The members were "protected" from the "lies and evils of the outside world." (It wasn't until my son came home that he found out that the Berlin Wall had come down several months before.) Instead, David would often show selected movies, and each would have a message. Most were "R" rated or war movies; few depicted life as it really is. Koresh used the movie plots to show his followers that they were just like the underdogs in the stories, and that through his leadership they would be victorious in the end receiving power, status and salvation.

Members were also encouraged to exercise; the women often did aerobics, while the men engaged in weight lifting.

The Waco Compound

After several weeks in California, Robert was invited to join other members in the group travelling to Waco, Texas, for two weeks of intensive training and "gathering for atonement."

Mt. Carmel was located on 77 acres several miles from Waco. It was very active with a great deal of construction underway. But Robert's schedule was set for intense instruction, which he received from David Koresh's parents.

David Koresh arrived the second week and took over the training, which filled every day.

It was during this time that Robert first overheard references to "Branch Davidians," although he was told personally that the group was not affiliated with any organized religion.

It was also during this time that Robert heard about "special studies" being given privately by David Koresh in his bedroom, or "the upper room" as he called it. In his naiveté, Robert hoped he would be chosen for a special study—others often waited hours for them.

He later realized what was happening when David Koresh announced in a "new light" revelation that all women belonged to him and him alone. From that moment on all men were to remain celibate. Husbands were to turn their wives over to David and receive their own "perfect wives" in heaven. There was no longer a need to be married while on earth.

This was another "last straw," which caused several couples to leave the group. Steve Schneider was one who found the teaching unbelievable. To get him to stay, David "anointed" Steve to a special position and gave him additional responsibilities. And after many persuasive talks, David convinced Steve and his wife to remain under the revised rules. As a result, their faith became even stronger.

Robert, meanwhile, spent all his free time concentrating on David's message, trying to understand what he was teaching, trying to be worthy so that understanding would come. He would hear David's voice over and over in his head. The more he tried to make sense out of David's messages, the more muddled he became.

He took long walks along the many trails at the compound, meditating on "the word," concentrating on David's teaching. On one of these walks, during a period of intense concentration, "my mind opened up and all of a sudden a million different thoughts came in at one time, kwish, right into my head. I guess it was bad stuff because it wasn't a fun experience. But I tried to look at it logically and try to think, 'What is this? What is happening to my mind?' And not being able to understand what is going on is what really made it hard."

Robert's escape from the Branch Davidians

Robert's episode in Waco was the beginning of his mental trauma. He began sensing an invisible entity trying to kill him.

"At first it was trying to get me to kill myself, to do it voluntarily through delusions. Not physically, but mentally kill myself, like no longer breathing, or just willfully stopping the heart. It was totally beyond anything I had ever felt before. And it was beyond scarey, it was terrifying. And I couldn't fight it because it wasn't something outside, it was something inside me that was trying to do this."

In his terror, Robert would panic and seek out others, hugging them and pouring out his grief. But others offered little or no consolation.

Eventually, Robert felt that the invisible "entity" would do the killing, but only at the time of its choosing. Meanwhile, it would constantly stalk him.

"I acted like, and I felt like, I was a person about to be killed. It had the ability to just stop my life. And it was beyond my control, often coming to me when I was about to fall asleep, then backing away again when I was wide awake. I constantly felt the hand of death on me."

After Robert was returned to California, he began hallucinating, seeing the world change into the Garden of Eden, which David Koresh promised it would, only to have it return to the "evil world of reality" before he could step out of it. Or laser beams would blast out from unexpected sources, aimed at severing his penis and splitting him into two sexless beings. And God lived beyond Uranus, waiting for events on earth to complete their designed course.

It was then that Robert was sent home to us to recover.

David Koresh reveals his hand

During the 3½ years it took for Robert to completely recover, I had several conversations with David Koresh. I felt that if I knew more about the group and the man that Robert was involved with, I could better help him recover.

The phone calls I made to David resulted more in frustration than resolve.

First of all, I never had the opportunity to talk to someone other than David. If someone else answered the phone, the second voice I would hear would always be David's. He would not tell me who else was in the group or if any others had suffered the same hallucinations that Robert had. He refused to talk about himself. He did state that the group was "not associated with any Christian organization," and it had no formal name. "We're just a bunch of young men who meet together occasionally for Bible study," he said.

David always talked to me in a very rapid-fire manner, and very quickly he would manipulate the conversation to talking about his "revelation knowledge," which I never could understand. He tried to convince me that he had the "truth" about God's word and that everything I had been taught all my life was a lie. He would not help me understand Robert's condition, how he got that way, or how he might be helped.

Although the talks with David Koresh did little in helping me with Robert's recovery, they did help me understand the man, his influence and his control.

During the 51-day standoff in Waco, Texas between the Branch Davidians and the federal agents of the Alcohol, Tobacco and Firearms (ATF), I felt I understood exactly what David Koresh was doing. The gentle but firm voice talking in circles was all too familiar to me. I know he relished the power of keeping the ATF at bay, wondering what his next move would be. And in a very real sense, he was controlling the FBI, the President of the United States, and the entire nation because he commanded the attention of the media. And I could almost hear him talking to his followers: "See, I told you they (the ATF) would do this, didn't I? They are exactly as I described them, aren't they? Now you believe I am who I say I am, don't you? They are the evil of the world, they have come to destroy us, and we shall triumph beyond the apocalypse!"

I was saddened for those who fell under his power and control.

My heart goes out to those federal agents who were killed or injured and their families and friends. I continue to grieve for everyone who died in the fire, but even more I grieve for those who survived the fire and are still caught up in the spiritual deception.

Resources

Organizations listed under the Secular heading investigate both religious and non-religious cults, and investigate both Christian and non-Christian religious cults. Organizations listed under the Christian heading investigate cults from a Christian point of view. Organizations listed under the Resource Referral heading do not specialize in cults but include cults in their overall research activities as listed.

Although many more cult resources are available nationwide, I can only recommend those on the following list. If you have any recommendations from your own experience, please write to me in care of the publisher.

—Alice Scott

Secular

American Family Foundation Information Service
P.O. Box 2265
Bonita Springs, FL 33959
(212) 249-7693 (New York Office)
Herbert L. Rosedale, President
Specializes in cults. Offers films, tapes, books, leaflets, lectures, referrals, *Cult Observer Journal* newsletter and *Cultic Studies Journal*, research findings. Because of budget restraints and staff size, further investigation of specific cults is limited. Both paid and volunteer staff.

Cult Awareness Network
National Office
2421 West Pratt Blvd. Suite 1173
Chicago, IL 60645
(312) 267-7777 (Hours: 9-5 CST)
Cynthia Kisser, President
Specializies in cults and the occult. Offers films, tapes, books, leaflets, lectures, counseling, support groups, research, library, referrals, annual conferences, *CAN News* newsletter. Researches further when contacted about specific cults. Both paid and volunteer staff. Offices in 19 cities (call for referrals).

Cult Hot Line and Clinic
Jewish Board of Family and Children's Services
120 W. 57th St.
New York, NY 10019
(212) 632-4640 (24-hour)
Arnold Markowitz, Programming Dir.
Specializes in cults and cult-related groups. Offers professional counseling, psychotherapy, and telephone consultation. Does not further investigate cults (helps more in the recovery process of family and ex-cult members). Both paid and volunteer staff.

International Cult Education Program
P.O. Box 1232 Gracie Station
New York, NY 10028
(212) 439-1550
Marsha R. Rudin, Director
Provides preventative educational material on cults in general, and ritual abuse. Offers video tapes, books, lesson plans for high school, reports, research articles. Does not research further but provides resource referral. Paid staff.

Religious Movements Resource Center
629 South Howes
Fort Collins, CO 80521
(303) 490-2732
Hal Mansfield, Director
Specializes in cults. Fluent Spanish. Offers film presentations, lectures, counseling, support group, research, library. They have a large network, which can further investigate specific cults. Both paid and volunteer staff.

Christian

Christian Research Institute

P.O. Box 500
San Juan Capistrano, CA 92693
(714) 855-9926
(800) 821-4490 (Bible Answer Man - 3:00-4:00 M-Th PST, radio broadcast)
(800) 443-9797 (credit card line only)
(714) 855-9926 (customer service line)
Hank Hannegraaf, President
Specializes in cults, apologetics, religious movements, occult, New Age, philosophies, aberrational Christian movements. Offers books, audio/video tapes, pamphlets, referrals, radio broadcast, free newsletter, quarterly publication *Christian Research Journal*. Catalog available. Researches further if warranted. Both paid and volunteer staff. Offices in 4 cities (call for locations).

Denver Seminary

Attn.: Gordon Lewis
P.O. Box 10,000
Denver, CO 80210
(303) 761-2482
Professor Gordon Lewis, President
Specializes in cults. Offers referrals, literature, recommended reading lists, and books. Prof. Lewis does this in his spare time and investigates as time allows. No staff.

Rivendell

11373 East Alameda Avenue
Aurora, CO 80012
(303) 364-0109 (7:30-6 M-F, 8-5 Sat.)
(303) 869-9080 (answering machine)
J. Timothy Philibosian, President
Specializes in cult apologetics, cultural apologetics. Offers films, tapes, books, film presentations, lectures, *Rivendell Times* newsletter. Only investigates if warranted. Both paid and volunteer staff.

Spiritual Counterfeits Projects

Box 4308
Berkeley, CA 94704
(415) 540-0300 (MWF 10 am - 4 pm)
(415) 540-5767 (access line M-Th 10-2, gives direct access to an SCP researcher; fluent Spanish, Korean)
Tal Brooke, President
Specializes in Eastern Religions, occult, New Age, cults in general. Offers films, tapes, books, leaflets, slide presentations, outreach, lectures, counselling, research, *SCP Newsletter*. Both paid and volunteer staff.

Resource Referral

American Religious Center

(National office)
P.O. Box 168
Trenton, MI 48183
(313) 425-7788 (main office)
(313) 347-3767 (public relations)
(313) 535-0842 (computer bulletin board)
Keith E. Tolbert, Director
Specializes in cults, occult, world religions, New Age, United Pentecostal Church International (Jesus only). Offers films, tapes, books, leaflets, computer programming databases, lectures, counseling, radio program, annual conferences, *ARC Update* newsletter, yearly publication of the *Directory of Cult Research Organizations* (worldwide listing of over 650 agencies and individuals who research and track cults). Researches cults as time and staff allows. Both paid and volunteer staff.

Commission on Cults & Missionaries
  Maynard Bernstein Resource Center
    on Cults of the Jewish Community
    Relations/Committee of the Jewish
    Federation Council of Greater L.A.
  6505 Wilshire Blvd, Suite 802
  Los Angeles, CA 90048-4906
  (213) 852-1234
  Terry Bell, President
Specializes in destructive cults and
missionary groups. Offers resource
materials, referrals, and public education programs. Does not research further. Both paid and volunteer staff.

Watchman Fellowship, Inc. —
    Birmingham
  P.O. Box 19416
  Birmingham, AL 35219
  (205) 942-4004
  Craig Branch, Senior Director
Specializes in cults, occult, campbellism.
Offers films, tapes, books, leaflets, film
presentations, slide presentations,
outreach, lectures, counseling, *The
Watchman Expositor* magazine. For
additional information, see Watchman
Fellowship — Arlington, Texas

For more information about herbal teas,
write to:

**Greater Cincinnati Nutrition
    Council**
  2400 Reading Road
  Cincinnati, OH 45202
  (513) 621-3262

Watchman Fellowship, Inc. —
    Arlington
  PO Box 13340
  Arlington, TX 76094
  (817) 277-0023 (M-F 9-5)
  (800) 669-2138 (for subscription to
    The Watchman Expositor)
  James Walker, Director
Specializes in new religious movements,
cults, occult, and New Age. Offers
lectures, witnessing materials, information, books, tapes, tracts, counseling by
appointment, *The Watchman Expositor*
magazine. Researches further if warranted. Both paid and volunteer staff.
Offices in 8 cities (call for locations).

Bibliography/Recommended Reading

Books

Breault, Marc and King, Martin. *Inside the Cult.* Penguin Books, 1993.

Cialdini, Robert B., Ph.D. *Influence, the New Psychology of Modern Persuasion.* W.W. Norton & Co., 1961.

Clark, J. G. Jr., et. al. *Destructive Cult Conversion: Theory, Research, and Treatment.* American Family Foundation, 1981.

Conway, Flo and Siegelman, Jim. *Snapping: America's Epidemic of Sudden Personality Changes.* J.B. Lippincott, 1978.

Enroth, Ronald M. *Churches That Abuse.* Zondervan, 1992.

Enroth, Ronald M. *The Lure of the Cults & New Religions.* InterVarsity Press, 1987.

Enroth, Ronald M. and Melton, J. Gordon. *Why Cults Succeed Where the Church Fails.* Brethren Press, 1985.

Frank, Jerome D. *Persuasion and Healing.* Schocken Books, 1974.

Fredericks, Carlton, Ph.D. *Psycho-Nutrition.* Grosset & Dunlap, 1976.

Gordon, Melton J. *Encyclopedic Handbook of Cults in America.* Garland Publishing, Inc., 1986.

Hassan, Steve. *Combatting Cult Mind Control.* Park Street Press, 1988.

Langone, M.D., Ph.D., *Cults: Questions and Answers.* American Family Foundation, 1988.

Larson, Bob. *Larson's New Book of Cults.* Tyndale House Publishers, Inc., 1989.

Lifton, Robert Jay. *Thought Reform and the Psychology of Totalism.* W.W. Norton, 1961.

Martin, Walter. *Kingdom of the Cults.* Minneapolis Bethany Home, 1985.

Miller, Maryann. *Coping With Cults.* Rosen Publishing Group, Inc., 1990.

Streiker, Lowell D. *Mind-bending.* Doubleday, 1984.

Magazines and Newspapers

Bordewich, Fergus M. "Colorado's Thriving Cults." *New York Times*, May 1, 1993.

Burtner, Father William Kent, O.P., interview with. "Don't Be So Sure You Could Say No To A Cult." *U.S. Catholic*, April 1990.

Harrary, Keith. "The Truth About Jonestown 13 Years Later." *Psychology Today*, March, 1992.

Safran, Claire. "Today's Cults Want You." *Woman's Day*, July 10, 1990.

A Note to My Readers

For several years I have loved and supported my son in his effort to undo the traumatic effects of just a few weeks of cult indoctrination. Over the last four years I have also talked to many survivors, and family members of survivors and victims of destructive cults. In each case the pain is very real. In each case the confusion and frustration is very real. In each case the recovery is very unpredictable and filled with relapses. And in each case I have felt the need for unshakeable love, understanding, caring, sharing, and most of all patience. Recovery is a long and arduous task for cult victims and families.

Through this book I hope to provide some answers and understanding of cults, how they function, and how they can be survived. But every cult experience is an individual journey and every journey unique. I would be very interested in hearing from anyone who has taken that journey, especially anyone who has used information in this book. What has helped you the most? What has helped you the least? Do you have any unanswered questions, or additional helpful advice? How could the book be improved? How could I help you better?

I also speak to organizations and support groups. Please write to the publisher for details. This book is used as a supplement in my talks. If you would like to order books for your organization at a discount, write to the publisher for a bulk order discount rate card. For individual books, simply fill out and return the coupon below.

—Alice Scott

Blue River Publishing Inc.
P. O. Box 6786
Colorado Springs, CO 80934-6786

Name	
Company	
Address	
City	
State	Zip
Phone	

Charge to: ❑ VISA ❑ MasterCard

Card expires _____

Signature _____

Blue River Publishing Inc.
P. O. Box 6786
Colorado Springs, CO 80934-6786

❑ Please send _____ copies of *"The Incredible Power of Cults"* at $9.95 each plus $3.00 shipping/handling.

Total for books	$	
Shipping/handling	$	
Colorado residents add 3% sales tax	$	
Total	$	

Books are shipped within eight weeks. **GUARANTEE:** If you are not completely satisfied with your books, return them within 60 days for a full refund.